SURVIVING SALESPEOPLE

THE MARKETER'S GUIDE TO WORKING WITH SALES TEAMS

TASHA HICKS

Copyright © 2020 All Rights Reserved.

No part of this book may be reproduced in any form or by any electronic or mechanical means including information storage and retrieval systems, without permission in writing from the author. The only exception is by a reviewer, who may quote short excerpts in a review.

The advice and strategies found within may not be suitable for every situation. This work is sold with the understanding that neither the author nor the publisher is responsible for the results accrued from following the advice in this book.

Edited by Gail Fay

designed by PartnerPeople, LLC

ISBN: 9798616465139

Independently published

Oceanside, California, United States of America

For Tom.
Thank you for always believing in me.

TABLE OF CONTENTS

Introduction   1

Part I
The Marketing/Sales Dynamic

Why Working with Salespeople Matters   9
Planning Your Strategic Relationship with Sales   17

Part II
Behaviors and How to Deal with Them

Behavior 1   Not Following Directions or Procedures   24
Behavior 2   Being Unresponsive   38
Behavior 3   Using Sales Techniques on You   45
Behavior 4   Not Reading Email   69
Behavior 5   Not Listening   81
Behavior 6   Nagging   88
Behavior 7   Oversimplifying   105
Behavior 8   Talking Too Much   112
Behavior 9   Sandbagging and Exaggerating   119
Behavior 10   Causing Schedule Problems   128

Conclusion   143

Acknowledgments 146
End Notes 147
About the Author 148

INTRODUCTION

I'm not going to tell you how great it is to work with salespeople.

It isn't.

If you're a marketing professional, chances are that you regularly interact with salespeople in your organization—and you know how exasperating it can be. You depend on them to help make your efforts successful, yet you have most likely experienced frustration because a salesperson didn't follow directions, didn't read an important email you sent, caused you to do unnecessary work, or even used a sales technique on you. The challenging, often antagonistic relationship between marketing and sales is well documented. But, to be truly effective in your role, you need to understand how to work with your company's sales team.

It's not as simple as learning to get along with salespeople or resolving to develop a happy cross-functional sales and marketing team. When you're working with salespeople, you're dealing with personalities and behaviors that are very different from those in marketing. By understanding the salesperson behaviors that cause the most frustration and by having tactics in place to anticipate and address those behaviors when encountered, you'll be better prepared to avoid irritation and get the results you need.

How I Learned to Work with Salespeople

I was lucky enough to start my marketing career working at an Apple sales office in Southern California. In this job I managed regional events and local trade shows, set up and promoted seminars, partnered with compatible software and hardware manufacturers to jointly promote solutions, and worked on local promotions and placed local advertising. At the time, I didn't appreciate the unique experience I had of starting my career as the marketing support person in a sales organization. Successfully working with salespeople was central to my job. I learned right away what I needed to do to communicate effectively with the team and to build a strong relationship with each field salesperson in the region. I later learned that my ability to understand and anticipate salesperson behavior while successfully carrying out my marketing objectives is a special skill.

I earned my MBA and moved into marketing roles at other companies, including both manufacturers and sales-centric channel organizations. I've worked in events, segment marketing, marketing programs, multichannel programs, alliances, product marketing, marketing communications, and management. I've also worked in sales organizations as a business development executive and inside sales manager, which has given me additional insight into typical salespeople personalities and the types of communication that works best to get their attention and compliance, as well as generate the best results to help me meet my marketing objectives.

How I Developed This Material

In preparation for writing this book, I talked to marketing and salespeople alike. Based on my own experience and observation, I assembled a list of frustrating (and typical) ways that salespeople act toward their coworkers. Then I talked to other marketing professionals and confirmed that my experiences mirrored theirs. I also interviewed sales representatives, sales managers, and sales executives, and I surveyed various non-sales professionals (engineers, accountants, attorneys, project managers, etc.). I categorized the salesperson actions that caused the most frustration into ten main behaviors. Finally, I noted what works best to achieve desired results when dealing with salespeople, what doesn't work, and why.

Through my interviews, surveys, and observations, I learned that no matter the organization, most sales reps act the way they do simply because they're salespeople, so there's no point in getting upset about it or trying to change their behavior. Rather, I learned it's more effective to understand their behavior and deal with it in a way that most efficiently achieves the results you need for your own success.

Not everything on my original list of frustrating sales behaviors made it into this book. The ten included here consistently rose to the top. For the most part, I learned how to deal with these sales behaviors the hard way: through experience and a lot of trial and error. As I discovered techniques that worked, I started sharing this advice with others. I have seen these ideas implemented effectively by people in various marketing roles, as well as by people outside of the marketing department.

Who Should Read This Book?

Because of my experience dealing with salespeople as a marketing professional, this book is written for marketers. However, I also received feedback from other departments—for example, engineering, tech support, legal, and operations—and these techniques can be used by professionals in these fields and more. Anyone who works with salespeople can benefit from this book.

If you are in marketing, you may infrequently work with salespeople in your current role, but as your career grows and your positions change, the odds are likely that successful interaction with your company's sales team will be critical to your success. Some of the marketing positions that regularly work with salespeople include the following:

> Trade show and events management
> Program management
> Product marketing
> Segment marketing
> Sales enablement
> Demand and lead generation
> Marketing communications
> Digital marketing
> Channel marketing
> Creative services
> Public relations

Of course, this is a partial list. No matter what position you're in now or where you see yourself in five years, understanding how to work with sales teams will give you a career advantage.

What This Book Is and Isn't

Over the years, I've often said there should be a guide to help marketers deal with salesperson behaviors, so I finally wrote it myself.

This book will help you recognize and successfully deal with ten of the most puzzling and frustrating salesperson behaviors. I've included real-life examples of these behaviors and their sub-behaviors as well as the specific, practical strategies you can use to avoid them altogether, successfully handle them when they do occur, and minimize your chances of navigating them in the future.

Most books that discuss the relationship between marketing and sales suggest aligning the two departments in more of a collaborative relationship. However, if you look beyond the team-building platitudes, these books place the bulk of the responsibility in achieving this unity on the shoulders of the marketing team.

This book doesn't give you, the marketer, team-building techniques or strategies to improve collaboration between marketing and sales. It doesn't explain what marketing can do to better support sales efforts. Rather, it's a practical survival guide for individuals in marketing who need to work with the sales team and still remain both productive and sane.

When reading this book, you'll recognize some of the frustrating sales behaviors, although you may not have put a name to them before. Now you'll be able to recognize and even anticipate them, and you'll have strategies to implement. By understanding these behaviors and following the advice in this book, you'll develop a better relationship with your sales team, save yourself unnecessary work and frustration, and be able to run more successful marketing programs.

I attended an industry marketing conference where I took part in a session with about seventy-five other people. A marketing director from another company stood up to address a question during the discussion, and in his comments, he literally called salespeople "evil." Needless to say, his reaction was extreme, and salespeople are definitely not evil, but many marketers end up feeling this way. If used, the tips in this book can keep your frustration with sales from escalating to this level and enable you to use the sales team more effectively to achieve better marketing results in less time.

PART I
THE MARKETING/SALES DYNAMIC

Why Working with Salespeople Matters

Three months into a new segment marketing manager position, I flew from California to Missouri to present the new marketing program and campaign I had been working on to my company's sales team. After arriving in Kansas City late in the evening, I spent a sleepless night at the Doubletree and made it to our downtown office by eight the morning, which felt like six o'clock because I was still on Pacific time.

Running on adrenaline and jittery from too much coffee, I stood in front of the salespeople assembled in rows of chairs in the company's training room. I wanted to do well. I wanted the sales team to like me. I wanted to impress my new boss. I was meeting most of the salespeople for the first time, and it was my first presentation to the assembled team. I felt certain that they would welcome the work I had done that had resulted in the new programs I was presenting and that they would be enthusiastic about using the new sales tools and sharing the updated messaging with customers.

I didn't get the reception I expected.

My first warning should have been that several members of the sales team were wearing black. However, I was from California, where it was completely normal for several people to wear black at an occasion other than a funeral without coordinating in advance. I didn't even notice the group wearing black until someone mentioned it after my presentation. I found out later in the day that the black clothing was worn out of protest.

Protest!

Apparently, the sales team assumed, before ever meeting me or hearing what I had to say, that my marketing programs were put together arbitrarily and that like past programs, they would make no sense and be a waste of their time. The salespeople had worn black to protest new marketing programs in general as well as the company's assumption that they as salespeople would take time and effort away from selling to support these programs. Before meeting me or hearing what I proposed, these salespeople—who were supposedly part of my team and on whom I depended to be successful in my new job—were already planning to avoid working with me and to boycott supporting my marketing programs.

Thankfully, when I gave my presentation that morning, I didn't know any of this. I was excited, upbeat, enthusiastic, and confident. I presented information about customer-focused market segment programs that I believed would resonate with the sales team's customers and help grow our company's market share. I presented information about our new campaign and showed what I thought were some compelling examples of new advertising that our New York–based agency had put together.

At the end of my talk, a salesperson raised his hand and asked why we didn't just do an ad with a simple and obvious message that he suggested on the spot. A couple of people verbalized their agreement with this suggestion. This is when I first realized I had an issue with sales team buy-in. As I was in town for a couple more days, I invited a few of them to a meeting the next day so I could conduct my own sales rep focus group with the intention of understanding why they were so disenchanted with marketing and why they were so resistant to supporting new marketing programs.

With some work, understanding, and implementation of techniques outlined in this book, I was ultimately able to understand the source of resistance and turn the situation around. The salespeople at the company went on to support my programs, and in the coming year we grew the company's business in my market segment by about 80 percent. I couldn't have realized this success without first getting the sales team on my side.

Why Read a Guide to Sales Behavior?

What runs through your head when you know you must depend on salespeople for the success of your marketing efforts? Does it make you nervous? Tense? Are you already annoyed with the fact that you'll have to deal with sales reps at all? If so, you're not alone. Nearly all marketing professionals experience some frustration when they reach the point in any given project where they must work with salespeople for their programs to be successful.

As a marketer, you likely have experience and expertise formulating strategies, developing content, building programs and campaigns, and taking new products to launch. As you've discovered, however, the final key to making your marketing efforts pay off and showing sales results ultimately depends on salespeople. Having your sales team want to work with you and even help you personally succeed can be what drives your marketing efforts to meet and even exceed expectations. Being able to work with salespeople on a personal level can translate into achievement and success in your individual projects and in your career. Most marketing professionals work with salespeople daily, and they generally like doing so. However, every marketing person I've talked to, interviewed, or surveyed has expressed at least some level of exasperation from this working relationship.

These frustrations often arise because the marketer is surprised by the salesperson's behavior and doesn't have a system in place to deal with it. Because success with sales is central to determining the success of the marketer's programs, the marketer must figure out how to successfully engage the sales team without becoming overwhelmed.

In this book I outline the top sales behaviors that frustrate marketers and other non-sales professionals, and I show you how to successfully address each of these behaviors. If you have worked with salespeople for any amount of time, many of these issues will be familiar. If you are just starting to work with salespeople, you will likely run into these issues as your working life progresses. Either way, you will benefit from learning to handle these issues now rather than through years of trial and error.

Whatever type of marketing you do and whatever your career trajectory, the integration of the sales team is essential to your success. Because they are in front of the customer, field salespeople often have credibility inside your company that marketing professionals don't. If you get in a battle with sales, they will probably win, even if they are wrong.[1] Your campaign delivery is likely carefully planned, yet the salesperson's motivation to help you achieve results is usually left to chance. The compliance and drive of any given sales individual may be critical to the success of your work, to the results you can demonstrate in your job, and even to the level of success you achieve in your career.

Salespeople are critical to you as a marketer, and to your company's marketing organization, in many ways; here are a few:

- Following up on leads generated by marketing

- Communicating with customers about programs, products, and promotions

- Staffing events that require salespeople to be available to talk to customers and prospects

- Driving their customers to attend customer-focused events such as seminars and customer-appreciation activities

- Providing contact information for customers who are willing to be the subject of a case study, provide a quote for marketing materials, or be a reference for other prospects considering doing business with your company

- Providing data so campaign results can be measured

- Ensuring successful implementation of CRM (customer relationship management) technology

- Providing accurate research results

What If You Don't Want to Work with Sales?

Salespeople are a key part of almost every company. As a marketing professional, especially in a B2B (business-to-business) environment, you have little choice but to work with them. Still, you may wonder if it's possible to avoid working with salespeople.

The answer is yes, kind of. In most organizations, there are professionals in marketing and other departments who avoid interfacing with the sales team. I've done it! I began avoiding one salesperson because he talked on the phone for so long. I'm still friends with this person and I enjoyed working with him, but I didn't have time to talk with him and still get my work done. So, I empathize with people who don't pick up their phone because they don't have time to deal with whatever the salesperson needs. But avoidance isn't something I condone, and it's not a solution. In fact, you can experience real opportunity-costs by doing so:

- You'll sacrifice your visibility within your organization, therefore limiting your chances for future promotion.

- You'll limit your network. At most organizations, the sales department has the highest headcount. As a result, it's possible that in the future, one of them may be working for a company you want to join. If salespeople you currently work with know you and like working with you, you'll likely have a ready network of people who can give you recommendations or referrals in the future. In addition, because salespeople are great networkers, they may be able to make introductions to people you want to meet when you're looking for a business solution or to expand your network.

- You'll put yourself at risk. Believe it or not, sales directors and VPs who have little experience in marketing—not marketing directors and VPs who have little experience in sales—are usually the ones promoted to VP of marketing and sales positions. Today's ambitious sales rep could one day be the person who is in charge of deciding whether your future marketing position is cut or retained.

- You'll hurt your reputation. If you actively avoid working with salespeople, or even if you just like to focus on your work and not go out of your way to work with the sales team, you may get a reputation as quiet, reclusive, introverted, or outright unhelpful. An article in Harvard Business Review states, "Senior managers often describe the working relationship between Sales and Marketing as unsatisfactory. The two functions, they say, undercommunicate, underperform, and overcomplain."[2] Because salespeople are so vocal, and because they talk to everybody, you need to manage how they perceive you. If you don't, they could express a negative opinion about you and hurt your reputation.

Planning Your Strategic Relationship with Sales

In most marketing organizations, you are typically left to develop your own strategy for handling the salespeople with whom you interact and on whom you depend for making your marketing efforts succeed. As part of your strategy, take time to plan for sales requirements, sales communication, and sales training. In addition, consider how the individuals in sales will react (or not react) to the materials, information, resources, and communication you provide as part of your marketing programs.

Even though salespeople want to achieve the same ultimate result as marketing—increased sales—they have different day-to-day agendas. These varying agendas result in different behaviors and reactions. As a marketing professional, you may be frustrated and surprised by sales' actions and find yourself asking, "Why don't they read their email? Why won't they follow up on these great leads? Why won't they reach out to their customer about creating a success story when they keep saying they need one? Why won't they follow a simple procedure that was put in place to help them?"

These different agendas and resulting behaviors contribute to the antagonistic relationship between marketing and sales. Marketing professionals often perceive salespeople as unreliable, apathetic, or even unprofessional. Salespeople often believe marketers lack understanding of sales processes and priorities. Often salespeople have short-term concerns, for example, making their immediate sales numbers, which will affect their next paycheck. As a result, salespeople prioritize these concerns over all others, even those that will make them more money in the long run. As a marketing professional, you will likely be developing customer communication materials and creating sales tools, customer-interaction opportunities, and even leads for your company's sales reps that could have amazing long-term sales results, while sales reps only wants to focus on what they need in the short-term. This difference in focus often results in a less-than-positive reaction by the sales team when marketing introduces new initiatives. If you know this up front, you can create a strategy ahead of time that will make your interactions with sales more productive and efficien and lead to your company's long-term success.

That's where this book comes in. It provides practical advice to help you deal with potential daily challenges you'll encounter while working with sales. Because achievement of marketing goals results in achievement of sales goals in the longer term, you will ultimately help bring salespeople in your organization more long-term success

Advantages of Working with Salespeople

Although this book primarily discusses how to identify and solve problems you may face when interacting with salespeople, that isn't to say that salespeople don't have positive qualities. Here are some of the top reasons marketers like working with salespeople.

They Possess High Energy and Passion

Many salespeople project energy and excitement about the projects and solutions they sell, their clientele, and the sales tools you may be providing. Their passion is often part of what makes them good at their job, and it has the added benefit of making them fun to work with. When someone is excited about the work you're doing, it's motivating.

They Achieve Results

If salespeople don't achieve results, they don't make their quota, and they don't get paid, so having them involved keeps your marketing programs results focused. I have seen marketing projects that are not sales focused go on for an infinite period of time without definitive results. In one case, a content replication program was set up, and when no one wanted to use it, the project turned into a series of activities designed to justify the existence of the content replication program. A program with sales involved would never get away with this. If something doesn't work, a sales team will drop it so they can move on to another activity that achieves results, that is, makes money. Because salespeople have this attitude, when you're working closely with them, you're more likely to show real results that translate into increased revenue for your company.

They Are Fun to Work With

While I have met one or two disagreeable salespeople, they are the exception rather than the rule. For the most part, salespeople are likable and personable. They make people around them feel comfortable and important. Because of their positive attitude, working with good salespeople can be energizing, motivating, and fun.

They Are Reachable

One of the things salespeople are good at is being available. They need to be reachable in case they are contacted by a customer; as a result, you can usually reach them if you need to. Whereas people on engineering, operations, legal, or other teams may be hard to get in touch with, salespeople will usually pick up the phone when you call—even if they are on vacation or at home.

They Are Easily Satisfied

I love creating materials that simply need the sales team's stamp of approval. If the copy works, they have no desire to rewrite it. They don't care if the background is red or blue or if I used a bold or narrow font. They don't care if the animated character in the product video is male or female, fat or thin. Most of the time, when I create any materials for the sales team, they are happy to go with it as long as it accomplishes the intended purpose. Because they are easily satisfied, it's possible to get a lot more accomplished quickly than it is when you work with someone from another department who may have numerous questions and revisions.

They Have Clear Focus

More than any other department, those in sales know exactly what they want, and their priorities are clear. Salespeople are driven to make money, period. Thus, when you're working with salespeople you know exactly where you stand. You can also be certain that if you develop a program that helps salespeople increase the size of their commission check, they will love working with you.

Their Insights Can Make You Better

Salespeople can help you focus your marketing efforts by letting you know what their customers are interested in and what features of your product or service will resonate the most. They can help you stay abreast of trends by communicating what they see in the marketplace. They can even give you insight into what they hear about the competition so you can be more proactive in your messaging.

Salespeople's Frustrating Behaviors

Although all of the above is true, this book isn't about how wonderful it is to work with salespeople. It's a self-help guide for identifying and working with the ten most frustrating salesperson behaviors:

1. Not following directions or procedures
2. Being unresponsive
3. Using sales techniques on you
4. Not reading email
5. Not listening
6. Nagging
7. Oversimplifying
8. Talking too much
9. Sandbagging and exaggerating
10. Causing schedule problems

Each of these behaviors includes subcategories of behaviors, some of which you'll probably recognize from your own work experiences. Along with describing these actions and reactions, I outline how you can anticipate these behaviors, avoid them if possible, address them when they arise, and even use them to gain the upper hand in your working relationships with salespeople. Additionally, I provide some examples from my own experiences and from the experiences of colleagues.

My hope is that you will use the information and methods ahead to avoid the stress that comes with this frustration, achieve more success in your work, and build a better relationship with your organization's sales team.

PART II

Behaviors and How to Deal with Them

Behavior 1
Not Following Directions or Procedures

I worked for a company that set up an annual award to send one non-sales professional—someone from the purchasing, finance, marketing, engineering, or other non-sales department—on the sales team's annual President's Club trip. Salespeople were asked to nominate non-salespeople for this award and then pick the person who had provided the biggest contribution to the sales team during the year.

To make a nomination, salespeople filled out a form that clearly stated they should nominate a person who was not in the sales organization and who was not commission based. Even so, every year, over 30 percent of the outside salespeople consistently nominated a commission-based inside sales representative, someone who was already part of the sales organization and thus already eligible for the regular President's Club trip. Despite receiving instructions for nominations during the weekly sales call and despite having the rules outlined in the email with the form attached, as well as at the top of the form itself, a third of the salespeople still didn't follow directions.

BEHAVIOR 1: NOT FOLLOWING DIRECTIONS OR PROCEDURES | 25

At another company we redesigned our business cards and had to get new cards for hundreds of sales reps quickly printed in the new design. To accomplish this in what we thought would be the easiest way, we sent all the salespeople a survey form with spaces for the normal business card information: name, title, address, phone numbers, and email address. We communicated to the salespeople that they needed to fill out their information on the form exactly as it should appear on their new business cards. By having the salespeople provide their information exactly as it should appear, we thought we could simply forward the file to layout and printing, thus saving an extra proofing step.

We were wrong.

About half of the salespeople responded with information formatted in a way that was clearly not how they would want it on their business card. There were abbreviations where there should have been full titles, titles that didn't make sense, first and last names that weren't capitalized, and even incomplete email addresses. As a result, we had to update and proof the information anyway.

What It Looks Like

Not following directions or procedures is the number one complaint marketing professionals have about working with salespeople. This problem can take multiple forms, from salespeople who never seem to learn how to use a function in your company's CRM tool to the sales reps who never seem to find a piece of literature on a cloud-based drive set up for their benefit, and thus contact you to get it emailed to them every time they need it.

Despite their apparent helplessness, salespeople aren't stupid. Sometimes, their end game is to do as little direction-following as possible and, instead, only spend their time doing work-related things that will help them to hit their next sales number and put immediate money in their pocket. So, sales reps will attend trainings, listen and even respond in a way that indicates they understand, and then go right back to doing things the way they have always done them or the way they would prefer to do them, despite whatever communication you have provided.

Taking the time to follow your marketing activity procedures isn't something salespeople perceive will help with their lives, careers, or wallets, so they don't want to encourage expectations that they will follow your procedures in the future. Sure, there are plenty of times when they aren't ignoring directions on purpose, but not following stated procedures is consistently the top complaint about working with salespeople.

I once worked on a project where the outside salespeople had to assign "customer type" categories to a short list of current customers. The customer type categories were defined and easily referenced on the document they were to work from. We did training, and we made the directions simple. One of these customer type categories was "new," and the definition of "new" in this case was that the customer was new to using the technology. (Granted, labeling the category "new to this technology" would have been clearer, but we were keeping

BEHAVIOR 1: NOT FOLLOWING DIRECTIONS OR PROCEDURES | 27

the category names very short and had a reference list of categories for the salespeople right on the document. And, since all the customers on the list were legacy accounts, it didn't make sense that "new" would mean anything other than "new to this technology.")

I went over the categorization instructions in a short live presentation to the sales team, and I also put all the instructions in an email. I sent them each a tailored document for their customers, so it would be fast and easy for them to work through their list. Even so, some salespeople absolutely could not follow these directions for categorization, especially pertaining to the "new" category. Ultimately, I had to change the category name to a longer one and go through it with some of the salespeople individually.

There are five sub-behaviors that fall into the category of not following directions and procedures.

Wanting You to Be Their Assistant

When salespeople convince you that they need your help with a procedure they could do themselves, they don't want you to give them a lesson in how to complete the activity on their own; rather, they generally want to hand it off and have you do it for them. Be careful of this. Good salespeople are adept at developing rapport, creating a sense of urgency, and convincing you to take on work even when it's not your job. You do not want to take on the role of their assistant. This undermines your authority, and they need to learn how to do the work for themselves.

Acting Like They Still Don't Understand

This is a follow-on to wanting you to be their assistant. When I think of this behavior, I remember my grandma acting like she didn't know how to pump her own gas at a self-serve station so she could get the attendant to do it. It totally worked. Like Grandma, salespeople may act like they don't know how to follow the directions or comply with the procedure so they can avoid doing it altogether.

I ran into this issue multiple times with the same group of salespeople when I was working on a CRM implementation project. After I explained to the salespeople as a group and then individually how to check new leads and log results, why they should do so, and what they would get out of it, the salespeople continued to claim they didn't know what to do. (Seriously, it was impossible that they didn't know what to do at that point!) "Playing dumb" was their strategy for not having to comply with the new CRM procedure.

Sales management kept telling me that the salespeople probably needed more training, but they had been trained multiple times; they really didn't need more training. The salespeople who "didn't get it" were generally top sales reps who could get away with ignoring some procedures if they wanted to. They never admitted they could follow the new procedures because if they did so even once, they would be held accountable going forward. In this case, the helplessness strategy worked for the top salespeople, and the VP of sales finally assigned a sales assistant to update the CRM for them. Good salespeople can be convincing. But when you know the individuals and begin to understand their motivation, you will detect when their helplessness is strategic.

Not Doing Anything

Another related behavior is not doing anything at all. This is often the case when salespeople are not following directions for activities like using CRM tools, providing customer data, following up on new leads, creating reports, and so on. Their default mode is often to not do work beyond what is absolutely necessary and what will help close sales in the short term. By not responding or acting, salespeople employ an avoidance tactic with the hope that if they avoid the task long enough, priorities will shift and the requirement will go away. To marketers, this inaction can appear as simply not following directions or procedures.

Requiring More (and More) Special Help

When salespeople need materials but won't follow procedures to get the needed materials on their own, they will keep contacting you if you're the person who helps them. Despite your job description and despite the resources available to the salespeople, if you're in the office and you pick up the phone, they will contact you for help. This can be frustrating and time-consuming, especially if you're the person who gave the directions or put the procedure in place specifically so that salespeople wouldn't have to keep coming to you. And despite your desire to do the right thing and help salespeople close a deal, doing so will only reinforce their behavior and lead to more of the same.

In coming to you for special help, salespeople are using the same technique on you that they would use at a customer location: they find a champion, and they leverage that person in the organization to make their job easier. Rather than learning what to do on their own and taking the time to comply with procedures in place, salespeople can now call you and have you take care of things for them because you are in the office, you are their designated champion (whether you know it or not), and you are responsive.

I recently talked to a successful sales team manager about this, and he explained that he always finds someone in the corporate organization to be his go-to person. "It doesn't really matter if the help I need is that person's job. The fact is that it's a person in that location that I can get ahold of who will help me track down what I need in order to get my deal done."

I do empathize with salespeople in the field; it is important for them to have someone in corporate who can support their efforts to get their job done. That said, it's equally important for you to have a strategy in place to deal with this issue so it doesn't become an ongoing problem for you. After all, you have a job to get done, too.

Being Hasty and Careless

I managed a trade show team for a computer peripheral manufacturer and had a small team of four people to set up and break down our trade show booth at the Consumer Electronics Show in Las Vegas. This is a big show, and we had at least a couple hundred pieces of equipment that needed to be

BEHAVIOR 1: NOT FOLLOWING DIRECTIONS OR PROCEDURES | 31

packed up at the end. While we had days to set up the booth and equipment before the show started, the break down had to be done quickly and we needed to get all the equipment packed up in one night. The expectation was that the salespeople working the show would stay after and help pack up. Having an extra ten people for a couple hours is a giant help in this situation.

As we neared the end of the show, the salespeople on the floor started getting antsy and shutting down equipment before the show was done. My team and I had to keep reminding them that the show wasn't over. It slowed them a little, but they didn't really listen. Once the show ended, they packed so quickly that when we came around to check we discovered that equipment was in the wrong boxes. For instance, each monitor was in a monitor box, just not the right monitor box—the model numbers and serial numbers on the boxes didn't match the equipment that was inside. So, on the last evening of the show, at the end of a very long day at the end of an extremely long week, my team and I had to pull all the packed equipment out of the boxes and re-pack everything because it had been packed too hastily by the salespeople who had stayed to help. It was frustrating, and it made for a long night with no sleep for me and the rest of my team.

Salespeople tend to be laser-focused on using their work time to find customers and close deals. That's pretty much the only thing that most of them are evaluated on, and they may discount other activity as superfluous to their job and so they seem to overlook details that we in marketing may consider important. Additionally, many of them have the perception that other people in the company must have the job of taking care of details, and because of this they don't need to worry about them. For instance, salespeople tend to abandon a room when a meeting is over without worrying about putting away materials they used, putting tables back in the original location, and pushing in chairs so that the room looks nice. They think someone else must be responsible for cleanup (no one officially has this job). Because they don't like taking the time to do it, they may hastily enter the minimum amount of data about a lead follow-up in your organization's CRM, and they won't worry about little things like capitalization or spelling errors. If hardly any prospects are walking through a conference that is still open, they want to pack up as fast as possible and get out of there regardless of whether the show floor is still open. These types of actions seem hasty and careless, especially to those of us in jobs that require meticulous attention to detail. The salesperson may think he is just trying not to waste time, or he may assume that someone else will come in after him and clean up the room, the data, or the hastily packed trade show materials. A slightly less generous observation is that he may feel roped into helping with something he doesn't care about, so he won't take the time to do it carefully.

How to Deal with It

With caller ID, it's now possible for salesperson-call-avoiders to never pick up the phone when a salesperson is calling. While this tactic seems to work in the short run, it's not a long-term solution for you or your organization. Plus, negative

BEHAVIOR 1: NOT FOLLOWING DIRECTIONS OR PROCEDURES | 33

consequences can result from avoiding a salesperson's calls. The worst likely short-term consequence is that the salesperson complains. Fortunately (or unfortunately, depending on your perspective), sales reps who complain do not usually draw much of a reaction from marketers and other managers in the corporate office. Most non-sales people outside of the executive suite will take everything a salesperson says with a grain of salt. Anyone who has worked with salespeople for any length of time has heard them complain about nearly every topic, justified or not. Because salespeople are generally persistent, however, they will find a work-around that may not comply with organizational procedures and cause more problems in the future.

So, if avoiding calls isn't the answer, what is? How can you deal with salespeople who ignore directions, don't follow procedures, and call you for more help? The following section suggests actions you can take to cut your losses in terms of wasted time or—ideally—increase the odds that people will pay attention and follow procedures in the future.

Manage Them Closely

If you need a specific salesperson to follow a procedure closely—for instance, completing a request for a trade show with sales justification or providing sales information that will affect your marketing results—one option is to manage him closely. This can be awkward because you aren't the salesperson's manager, and he doesn't report to you. The salesperson won't be affected by the kind of job he does for you, or by your feedback about the quality of his work. If the job requires the salesperson to be meticulous and careful, you must supervise him in a meticulous and careful way, and this creates more work for you. However, if the results are important, it is worth spending the extra time up front to ensure the input is correct the first time.

One way to manage a salesperson's activities closely is to give one or two directions at a time. After the person follows that part of the procedure, check the results before you move the person on to the next steps. Check the person's work every time and assume that if you don't, the process probably won't be done correctly. If the salesperson does everything right, that's fabulous. If she doesn't, you'll catch mistakes sooner rather than later.

Dismiss Them from the Activity

Taking the time to ensure that salespeople follow directions and correctly perform a task may be such a hassle that it's not worth it to you. If this is the case, you do have the option of simply dismissing them and doing the work yourself or with your own team. For instance, if you are packing up a small event or trade show and you or your team can do the packing in a relatively short period of time, you may want to tell the salespeople to go home. Having them stay after the event to "help" may take longer and be more difficult than doing it on your own because you will have to supervise as well as pack.

Make It Personal

When resistance to following directions or procedures is accompanied by a request for, or the assumption of, special treatment because of their friendly relationship with you, use the friendly relationship to your own advantage. Make the reason the salesperson needs to follow the internal procedure personal. Explain to the individual that going around the procedure will impact you personally by compromising your job, potentially costing you a bonus, or hurting the results of your reports to management. The salesperson will have no choice but to go back and follow directions if she wants to demonstrate that she is indeed your friend and doesn't want to hurt your position at the company.

Refer Them to the Correct Procedure

If a salesperson comes to you for help instead of following the established procedure, the best approach is using a standard reply referring him to the correct procedure—even if the request is something within the scope of your department or job. For example, if a salesperson asks you to help him download literature from a cloud-based site or check a calendar for event details—actions the person should be able to do for himself—tell him where he can find the correct procedure, but don't do it for him. By doing this, you avoid reinforcing the disruptive behavior that unnecessarily takes up your time and the time of your team, and you give the salesperson direction that enables him to be self-sufficient in the future.

Even if it's only one or two sales reps who are contacting you about an issue, it's better to send what looks like a standard or generic reply than to send a custom, individualized response. This way, the salesperson won't keep contacting you and expecting an individual reply. You can create an automatic reply, a form, a link, a standard email template, a signature response, a ticket, verbiage that you just copy and paste—whatever works for you. Most types of requests will come up over and over, maybe for years. So, be prepared with standard responses that redirect salespeople to follow procedures that make them self-sufficient. You'll be able to achieve more and spend less time helping them or giving them individualized directions.

Refer Them to the Correct Person

When salespeople repeatedly contact you to be their "helper" for something that's outside of your job scope, firmly let them know who they should contact and then hand them over to the right person. Do not take it on yourself to help them with something that's not your job or you will be contacted by the salesperson every time they need help with that activity, and possibly all kinds of activities. Set up a conference call with the salesperson and the correct contact, and make sure the sales rep has a warm, live introduction. This live introduction also ensures that the correct contact person doesn't just avoid the salesperson's call.

For email requests from salespeople, use the same tactic. Forward the email to the correct person, copying the salesperson and the explaining that you are not the correct

BEHAVIOR 1: NOT FOLLOWING DIRECTIONS OR PROCEDURES | 37

person but he or she is copied on this email.

You may need to repeat this action a couple of times or a ridiculous number of times, either because the salesperson keeps coming back to you or the correct person is unresponsive, which may be why the salesperson contacted you in the first place. The repetition required can be frustrating for all, but it's still preferable to falling into the trap of supporting the sales rep for items outside of your normal job scope.

Call Them Out

One way to prompt salespeople to follow procedures is to make information about their actions public and report it in a way that will make them uncomfortable if they are called out as not having performed the desired action. I had an issue getting sales reps to follow through on updating their data in a CRM system so that we could ensure our customer data was accurate. I asked them to make the updates multiple times and in multiple ways without results. I even got their managers involved but it had almost no effect. Finally, I created a report that called out the names of salespeople who hadn't updated data, and executives saw the report on a weekly basis. The salespeople couldn't be mad at me because the reporting system simply called out the existing data, and I couldn't change the data. Having their individual names viewed internally by executives every week made not taking action so uncomfortable that they finally chose to get the work done.

Behavior 2
Being Unresponsive

Crickets. That's what I got.

I had attended a large company sales meeting where a salesperson asked to have more customer case studies. Practically the entire sales force joined the chorus and expressed how much they wanted to have more case studies in their arsenal of sales tools. I stood up in front of the entire group, their managers, the sales VPs, and the CEO and explained that we in marketing would be excited to work on creating customer case studies. I also explained that to do this, we would need the sales team to identify the customers who would be candidates for the case studies and then make the customer introductions. One sales VP chimed in and made sure the reps were listening and that they understood they would need to reach out to their customers and respond to us in marketing to get any new case study production underway. After the sales meeting I sent out a follow-up email to the sales team with instructions about how to engage so we could produce the new case studies.

After the conference, however, I got crickets. No one responded. I followed up with the sales team in a group email to remind them of what I needed to create the case studies they had asked for. I called in to their weekly sales meetings to reiterate, and I still got no response. To finally push the sales team into action, I had to approach it in a way that would affect them more and be more visible (more on this technique in the Create Actual Visibility section).

What It Looks Like

In the preceding example, unresponsiveness took the form of not providing the requested information. None of the salespeople wanted to take responsibility for getting the work done, even though they all knew someone on their team would have to submit information before the case studies they requested could be produced. They all kept quiet in the hope that someone else would take on the work.

Lack of responsiveness applies to all sorts of activities, from responding to an inquiry about their attendance at the sales conference or customers' attendance at an event to feedback on lead follow-up or pre-orders of new product samples. The bottom line is that you don't receive the response that you requested.

There are multiple explanations for lack of salesperson responsiveness, ranging from ignorance of the response requirement to a desire to test the limits of how much they can avoid doing. It's hugely frustrating to be a marketer who needs sales response to get a job done and to be unable to get that needed response so you can complete your project

How to Deal with It

If a salesperson's inaction isn't visible to others—management, executives, or peers, for example—or if the salesperson simply perceives her unresponsiveness is invisible, the likelihood of that person responding to you is low. To combat this real or perceived lack of visibility, you have a couple of options:

- You can create actual visibility and include the salesperson so she sees how she is being viewed by others. As a result, the salesperson will want to change the way she is being seen.

- You can create perceived visibility, which will cause the salesperson to think her actions are, or will be, viewed by others in the organization. As a result, the salesperson will want to change the way she is potentially being seen.

In both cases, you can use a "carrot" approach, which employs positive reinforcement to encourage the desired behavior, or you can use a "stick" approach, which employs negative reinforcement to increase the frequency of a desired behavior while bringing about the termination or withdrawal of some aversive condition.[3] Both actual visibility and perceived visibility can be combined with a carrot or stick approach, depending on your circumstances and what you think will work best. Here's a breakdown of each of these four factors.

BEHAVIOR 2: BEING UNRESPONSIVE | 41

Create Actual Visibility

This approach involves creating actual visibility to the sales reps' inactivity and sharing that information with others in a highly visible way. In the case study example at the beginning of the chapter, this might involve creating a grid with all the salespeople's names and then sending out a communication to the whole team and to management showing who has and hasn't responded. Anyone copied on the communication can view the results, so this creates actual visibility of salespeople's actions.

Using a method that creates actual visibility results in scenarios such as the following:

- When they act in the desired manner, salespeople receive positive reinforcement from those who see the report. This coincides with the carrot approach.

- When they do not show a good result on the report, salespeople receive negative feedback. This coincides with the stick approach.

- Competition is created in the sales group. Since salespeople can see how all their peers are doing and all their peers can see how they are doing, competition naturally arises among the sales team.

Create Perceived Visibility

This approach involves creating a scenario that makes salespeople believe they will be perceived in a certain way, whether or not it actually happens. If salesperson behavior changes as a result of creating perceived visibility, you will not have to escalate information to management and create true visibility.

When I attended a weekly sales meeting without executives and showed the sales reps a report that highlighted those who had a large backlog of leads that hadn't been followed up on, I created perceived visibility using the stick approach. The sales reps who were caught up with their leads didn't appear on the report, but those who were behind looked really bad, and they knew it. I hadn't actually showed the list to management, but the sales reps on the report could envision what would happen if I did. Because they didn't want to look bad in front of the executives and receive uncomfortable attention, these sales reps changed their behavior without me having to escalate the report to management. The salespeople changed their behavior through perceived visibility alone. As a result, I looked like a genius for getting salespeople to change their behavior without involving management, and I was even offered a promotion.

Use a Carrot Approach

This approach involves rewarding responsive salespeople in a visible way so they continue the desired behavior. People respond extremely well to positive reinforcement. When one salesperson responds in a way that you want to reinforce and replicate in others, offer a big pat on the back in front of all their peers or their boss. For instance, if a couple of salespeople step up and provide you with customer contacts for the production of case studies, you might send an email out to the whole organization that says something like this:

> *A big THANK YOU to Shane Downey and Mary Watson who stepped up and helped the whole team by providing customer contacts for our case study project. You are both AWESOME! Here's the list of sales reps and customers who are currently participating.*

This approach to positive reinforcement uses visibility to influence salespeople who already responded to respond even more, and it also makes the unresponsive sales reps want to respond so that they receive the same kind of public positive attention.

Use a Stick Approach

This approach involves getting salespeople to take action to avoid a negative consequence. If you have a way to make salespeople more uncomfortable by not doing something than they would be by doing it, you can use a stick approach to deal with their lack of responsiveness.

For example, you could create a report for a weekly management meeting that shows the salespeople who have not followed up on their leads. Salespeople will suffer a negative consequence if they are on the list. You could also send a group email calling out items you need from salespeople or sales teams:

- We need confirmation from the San Diego branch as to whether May 18 is an approved date for the medical solutions seminar.

- We need names of customers attending from all sales reps before we can distribute tickets for the golf tournament. We are still waiting for this information from
    - Matthew Burman
    - Lyle Hughes
    - Shayla Johnson
    - Felix Hanson

Behavior 3

Using Sales Techniques on You

> *"Can you send me the most updated literature and presentation slides for our white-glove installation service? I am presenting the solution to the largest school district in the state tomorrow, and if they like the installation solution it will seal a million-dollar deal."*

When I saw this request from one of my company's top sales reps, I felt a wave of alarm. I had heard of the installation service, but it was still new, probably still in the pilot phase. We hadn't created any literature for the solution, and we definitely didn't have presentation slides. But somehow this salesperson had assumed we had created these collateral items, and he needed them for an important presentation that could be a big win for the company.

Creating messaging and collateral for new solutions typically went through product management and took time to create. Rushing to get the salesperson what he needed for the sales call would mean I would have to drop everything and track down people who could help me understand the solution well enough to write copy that same day. Plus, I would have to create the slides and lay out the literature myself—or else bribe one of the people on the creative team to help me.

Responding with "Sorry, we don't have those yet" would turn me into the bad guy. The salesperson could escalate to his management the fact that he didn't have what he needed from marketing. If he lost the sale, the rep could blame it on the fact that he didn't have any material or information about the installation solution, so the customer would think our service was only half-baked. My only choice was to get the sales rep what he needed, so I responded that we didn't have what he was asking for, but I would work on getting him what he needed for his sales call.

For the next twenty-four hours, I dropped everything else to ensure the rep had what he needed for his important presentation. I tracked down the details of the solution by having a call with the company we used to provide the white-glove solution. Fortunately, someone I had worked with previously at a different company worked there and took the time to help me understand the details of the solution and get all the information as well as some photos. I laid out literature myself using a template, and I created PowerPoint slides the salesperson could use in his presentation to the school district. I stayed at the office and worked late into the night to get everything done before the next day. I missed my train and had to make the long drive home in the old car I kept at the train station. I didn't get much sleep, and I still remember being very tired the next day as I came in to catch up on the work I had dropped in order to attend to the salesperson's emergency project.

I learned later that while the salesperson was calling on the school district, it wasn't a critical presentation that would make or break a million-dollar deal. The salesperson knew we didn't have material for the white-glove installation solution yet, but he had framed his question in a way to make me think we should. He wanted to have materials to help him talk about the new solution at the sales call, so he used sales techniques to manipulate me into finding a way to provide him with the materials he asked for.

What It Looks Like

Yes, salespeople use sales techniques on their coworkers, especially those in marketing. While I've always known this behavior was frustrating, in doing research for this book, I learned that it happens all the time. Among the marketing professionals I interviewed and surveyed, this behavior was listed as one of the three most frustrating, with a third of the respondents noting that it was one of the things they most dislike about working with salespeople.

Because salespeople at your company are your coworkers, you may not always be looking out for their use of sales techniques. When you recognize after the fact that a salesperson has used a sales technique on you, you may feel frustrated and angry at being manipulated. The only way to address this issue is to learn to recognize sales techniques your coworkers/salespeople are using at the time they are using them. Then you can weigh the likelihood that they are trying to influence you with sales techniques and decide whether to reprioritize your regular work based on their request.

Different techniques work for different salespeople, so they vary by person and situation. The following list includes the most common internal sales techniques, though there are certainly others.

Urgency

The story at the beginning of this chapter is an example of urgency combined with a threat of negative consequences and an assumptive close (both of which are discussed in the following sections). Urgency is used commonly by salespeople, to the endless frustration of those of us who work with them. This is the phenomenon where a sales rep tells you something must be done by a certain time to meet a deadline for a meeting, conference, presentation, or other event. I am not exaggerating when I tell you that at least half the time I've rushed to get something done for a salesperson, I discovered later that the individual didn't even use it for the indicated activity or didn't need it by the stated deadline.

While urgency nets a positive result for the salesperson because her project is done right away, it can be extremely

BEHAVIOR 3: USING SALES TECHNIQUES ON YOU | 49

frustrating for you and have negative consequences that affect the rest of your professional and personal life. Other urgent projects may get put aside or hastily completed, you may spend extra resources to rush design work and printing, and you may end up working extra hours and missing your daughter's band performance or postponing a night out with your spouse.

Threat of Negative Consequences

This sales technique builds on urgency. Whenever salespeople tell you that their deal hinges on whatever it is they are asking you to do in a rush, they are using the threat of negative consequences. The project could be anything from creating an updated price list to printing a new brochure to helping them complete a response for a customer RFP (request for proposal). This sales technique creates the element of fear in you—that you could be the reason the company loses a deal. It can have the same results as urgency: other projects get rushed or pushed aside and you end up working extra hours to get the salesperson what they say they need in their hurried time frame.

This is also a tough one to deal with because you don't want to be blamed for losing a sales deal. In my experience, however, when a sales rep uses the threat of negative consequences to influence you to prioritize what he wants done, the consequence is generally exaggerated.

Liking, Friendship, Exclusivity, and Similarity

These four techniques are slightly different but fall into the same category of relationship building. Salespeople use these techniques all the time in the office, and these behaviors come naturally to most good salespeople.

I worked for a company for more than five years where I had a great relationship with one of the top salespeople. She asked me to lunch all the time, she invited me to parties at her house, she brought back souvenirs from trips, she would come into my office to talk, and I asked her advice about how to work with certain people she knew well. In short, we were friends. Then I switched companies and it stopped. It wasn't that she was rude or unfriendly or anything like that—quite the contrary. I saw her at other events where I was a plus one, and she was just as friendly and charming. But I was no longer part of her job, so she moved along to focus on the relationships that would help her career. She was a great salesperson and had formed the friendship with me because it made her job easier. When the friendship no longer served the purpose, it wasn't the best use of her time. She needed to cultivate a friendship with the next person who could help her. Her actions didn't upset me because I recognized that she was a great salesperson using a sales technique and that she was singularly focused on being the best at her job. When the sales technique was no longer necessary, she stopped using it.

Here's a summary of the four relationship-building sales techniques:

BEHAVIOR 3: USING SALES TECHNIQUES ON YOU | 51

- Liking: When salespeople use this technique, they literally let you know that they like you. They might say things like "You're the best!" "You rock!" or even "I like you!" It's a simple and effective technique.

- Friendship: As mentioned, salespeople use friendship as a sales technique, and the friendship may very well be genuine. A certain salesperson may come by your office to chat, go to lunch with you, or even do activities outside of work.

- Exclusivity: When salespeople use this technique, they share information with you that is not for public consumption in an effort to develop an "exclusive" and special relationship with you. For example, a salesperson might give you access to something that's special or limited edition, like taking you backstage before a show where their customer is an event venue. Or a salesperson might share gossip about other people in the company, tell you something personal about himself, or even tell you an inappropriate joke that couldn't normally be shared in the workplace.

- Similarity: To build a relationship, salespeople will sometimes focus on similarities they share with you, anything from a similar name or hometown to personal or professional interests you have in common.

The Assumptive Close

The "assumptive close" sales technique is sometimes called the "secondary question" close or "thinking past the sale." This technique is well-known and is commonly taught in sales training classes. In my experience, it's often used by sales managers.

When employing the assumptive close, salespeople will communicate in a way that assumes you are already doing something. They don't directly ask if you are taking or have taken a certain action. Instead, they ask a secondary question that assumes the first action has already taken place. The idea is to make you think that you are supposed to be doing something or that you forgot to do something, and that you better get it done before anyone notices.

I worked at a company where one sales manager in particular used this technique with people on my team. For example, she would say something like "When are you going to have that landing page done?" Her question assumed that the marketer was already working on the landing page and asked when it would be done. My marketing team member would be caught off guard, thinking he had forgotten about the landing page and would rush to get it done before anyone noticed. In reality, the sales manager's question was the first time my team member was hearing about the project, but he would question himself because it seemed like something he should have known about. The sales manager used the technique to shortcut internal project request processes and get her items prioritized and done quickly.

Mirroring and Leading

Mirroring is a way of developing rapport rapidly and is based on the principle that people like people who are similar to themselves. This is a classic technique that most salespeople either use, have had training in, or have at least some awareness of how it works. Some sales reps are so accustomed to using mirroring that they will do it automatically when they meet with you.

When using this technique, salespeople will mimic your body language: crossing their legs the same way, leaning back or forward when you do, or holding their head or arms in a similar way to yours. They may also mimic your voice and your speaking tempo and volume. Some even go so far as to slightly mimic your accent if it's different from theirs. They may pick up on your communication and processing style, for instance, getting right to business if you don't like to chit-chat, or taking a minute to make small talk if that's what you normally do.

This technique works on a subconscious level and is well outlined in sales books and by neurolinguistic programming practitioners.[4] Once a salesperson has used mirroring with you, you will subconsciously begin to mirror and match his actions and/or speech. At this point, the salesperson has developed a rapport with you such that he can more easily get you to agree or do what he is asking of you by "leading" you, or getting you to start following his actions. For example, a salesperson who has established rapport like this might nod when he is talking to you as a way of getting you to automatically say "yes."

Social Proof

This technique involves explaining that you should do something a certain way because another respected company is doing it, and so it must be acceptable, effective, competitive, or important. The principle of social proof states that one means we use to determine what is correct is to find out what other people think is correct.[5]

I once had a situation where a salesperson wanted to run a contest, which was really a sweepstakes (if you have ever had to run one of these, you'll understand that the verbiage is important because of the legal meaning of contest or sweepstakes). People could enter to win new equipment for their office. I explained that there were strict rules around sweepstakes that we would have to comply with. His response was that another well-known company—one of the top three in the industry—was doing it without following these same rules, so it must be okay. Of course, I didn't just go ahead with the sweepstakes without following appropriate rules. I instead worked with our legal department to make sure we were in compliance and also made sure that the sweepstakes was only promoted to the types of customers who would be able to accept the prize. It took longer to implement than the salesperson would have liked, but we did it right and it had a positive result.

It's very tempting to follow the example of a respected company you assume does everything correctly and has nothing but successful programs. However, respected companies have ineffective and costly programs all the time. I've seen some of them up close. For instance, I remember an expensive social media campaign targeted at IT managers that had almost no results. I also recall a great print advertising campaign that didn't help to move sales of a new product at all.

Reciprocation

Reciprocation is the concept of "I've done something for you, so you should do something for me." It's the reason why sales reps bring muffins to clients on Friday mornings or give presents to clients at holiday time. It doesn't seem like these actions should really influence sales, but they do, and for some people, the pull to reciprocate when they have been given anything is extremely strong.

The "rule for reciprocation" says that we should try to repay, in kind, what another person has provided us.[6] Salespeople often use this technique on their coworkers in marketing. They may bring you a small gift, a trinket from a customer location, donuts on Friday morning, or a cutout of an ad they think will interest you. Reciprocation also works for more abstract concepts. For instance, if the salesperson arranges for you to get a quote for the website from one of her clients, she believes she has done something for you and you will be more likely to put her requested collateral at the front of the line. Other examples include the sales rep telling you that she said something positive about you to an executive or that she gave you credit for something in a presentation. With reciprocation, salespeople expect that any action on their part that benefits you will result in you giving them favorable or preferential treatment.

Perceived Authority

In an effort to secure prioritized, preferential treatment from marketing, sales managers can act as if they have authority over marketers in their own company. For example, these managers might give assignments, ask for progress updates, and generally communicate with marketers in a way that puts them in charge.

I've received this treatment from both male and female sales managers. At one company, right after my introductory email went out, I received a note from a sales VP requesting an introductory call. I expected a friendly conversation where he would explain the details about his team and their focus. Instead, he handled the call as if he was my manager, asking me to go over my priorities and projects as if I reported to him. I had a clear set of priorities, and it was easy for me to go through them. Once I was through reviewing this information, the VP tried to give me an assignment, telling me I should focus on a data project that was obviously a priority to him but not one of the priorities I had been given by my own manager. While I made a note of his issue, I didn't commit to working on it. The sales VP wasn't my boss, and while it was great to know about issues he believed needed addressing, it wasn't his place to give me an assignment, and it wasn't my place to accept an assignment from him. While he was behaving as if he had authority, he really didn't.

Although it was tempting to get his immediate approval by agreeing to work on his project, I held my ground. I was friendly and upbeat, I thanked him for the information, and I said I would review it with my new manager. Being new with the company, the last thing I wanted to do was to be perceived as abrasive or unfriendly, but I also didn't want to start the work relationship as one where I would readily accept that he had authority to tell me what to work on. When I met with my boss, I mentioned the sales VP's data project, and it turned out to be a completely unnecessary activity for me because it was being taken care of another way. It didn't come up again.

You've probably encountered perceived authority from experienced salespeople and sales management in your own organization. When salespeople act as if you work for them, especially if they have a title that outranks yours, tenure with the company, or status because of their sales numbers, they are using perceived authority to get you to prioritize them and their requests. Believing the perceived authority of salespeople and sales managers can distract you from your priorities, take up your time, and frustrate you and your manager.

Why is it so important to be aware that you are in a situation where you are being influenced by authority, real or imagined? Because authority has such strong influence that under certain circumstances, you can find yourself acting against your better judgment.[7] Social psychologist Stanley Milgram, a Yale University researcher, performed one well-known study of using authority as an influence.[8] Milgram conducted experiments that measured people's willingness to obey someone they perceived as an authority figure, which in this case was just a person in a lab coat with a clipboard. People were asked to deliver increasingly high shocks to another subject on the opposite side of a wall when that subject answered questions incorrectly. Within an hour, the shocks people were told to give the subject were high enough to be deadly. The people being asked to give the shocks were aware the level was dangerous and even deadly. An astonishing percentage of people complied with the instructions to shock the subjects on the other side of the wall: half of the male students and all the female students continued to do as they were told, even as they were simultaneously protesting and weeping for the person they were shocking. As this study showed, even a small amount of perceived authority caused more than half the people in the study to commit what would have been a deadly act.

This sales technique, especially when used within an organization, is incredibly manipulative. It's not your job to report to sales, and although the sales team may be your customer, you don't work for them. It's very easy to be influenced by perceived authority, so keep your job and your priorities in perspective and do not be afraid to push back when anyone besides your own management starts giving you assignments.

Repetition

Repetition is the idea that the more times you hear or see something, the more important it becomes. As marketers, we are familiar with this concept. We know that by citing a specific metric or feature multiple times, the data becomes more important because people are thinking about it. For

BEHAVIOR 3: USING SALES TECHNIQUES ON YOU | 59

instance, if you're looking for a computer display and you see five-bullet specification lists that compare response time on all the displays at the store, suddenly response time will be important to you in your display selection, even if you've never heard of it before.

Salespeople often use repetition by bringing up something they want multiple times to multiple people. They will mention it to you, your boss, management, coworkers, and anyone else at your company who may have influence. Suddenly, even if the item should be low on your marketing priority list, the sales team's agenda will float to the top because multiple people within the company are now thinking about it. Because sales has repeated the issue to multiple people, it will become classified as important.

If a salesperson keeps asking you about the same item or project even though you have already communicated the status, he or she is probably nagging instead of using repetition. If this is the case, skip to Behavior 6: Nagging.

How to Deal with It

When salespeople use sales techniques to get you to prioritize their projects, they turn everything into a fire drill—a situation where you need to drop everything else and focus on the new activity. Learning to recognize how and when the most common sales techniques are used in the office will help you respond appropriately, keep your true priorities at the top of your to-do list, and stay out of fire-drill mode as much as possible.

Listen and Ask Questions

Listening and asking questions are your primary tools for dealing with urgency, threat of negative consequences, and the assumptive close. All three of these techniques are based on some type of exaggeration, so by learning what is truly required (and not required), you can understand what is really necessary and in what time frame.

- Urgency

Addressing urgency can be challenging. We want to take salespeople at their word when they say they need help. Plus, no one wants to get in the way of a sales opportunity. I certainly don't.

To deal with urgency, listen carefully to the request and ask the salesperson questions about the specifics of the project and about the activity causing the urgency. For instance, what is the specific event for which the sales rep needs the new literature printed, and what day does it actually start? Does the rep really need the entire quantity, or is it possible to design or print a partial amount? Is the meeting external or internal? Finding out this information will tell you whether the expedited scenario is real and give you a minimum acceptable quantity so you don't unnecessarily complete the entire project on a rush deadline. Let the salesperson know what you can and can't do in his time frame, and what the real time frame will be to get everything he wants without compromises. If the content or quality is more important than the deadline, the salesperson may back off.

- Negative Consequences

As with urgency, the best way to deal with the threat of negative consequences is to ask detailed questions and find out as much as possible about the request, who it's for, and the consequences that may or may not result from your actions. Leverage what you already have on hand as much as possible and provide the salesperson with a breakdown of what you can and can't do in her indicated time frame.

In addition, take note of who is using the threat of negative consequences, because salespeople who use this technique are likely to use it more than once. I'm not suggesting that you avoid working with these people in the future, but that you approach working with them differently. When someone has used this sales technique on you in the past, be quicker to question the legitimacy of the request deadline and the potential negative consequences, and take a harder line when communicating how much time a project will take. The person likely won't change her "urgency" approach, but by keeping your boundaries clear, you can protect yourself from the undue stress that comes along with consistently tight deadlines.

- Assumptive Close

The assumptive close, also known as the "secondary question close" or "thinking past the sale," is designed to put you on the defensive and leaves you scrambling to complete a project you think you should have had on your to-do list but didn't. To deal with this technique, first verify you are being asked a secondary question that assumes an action on your part. These questions are often worded as "When will that task be done?" rather than "Are you working on that task?" Second, when you realize a salesperson has asked a secondary question, don't immediately jump to do what the person expects you to do. Instead, respond with questions about what the person is assuming, for example, "Where did you get the idea that I was working on that task?" Even if their assumed close is something you could do quickly, it's better not to set the salesperson's expectation that she can easily use the technique on you or your team.

Here's an example: Let's say a salesperson asks when are going to send him a sell sheet that you haven't created and that you don't remember being asked to create. Pause for a second to think about what the salesperson is asking. Do you remember being asked to create this sell sheet? If not, ask the salesperson "When was that request made? Who made it?" If you're sure no request was made, you could respond with something like "I don't have a record of that request, so it must be new. Can you please submit the request for the sell sheet via our regular ticket process?"

If the salesperson "assigns" a project you have a reason for not doing, explain why the project isn't done and how the rep can request it if needed. For instance, if the salesperson says, "Can you send me the price list that has only list prices?" and there's a reason you don't have a price list like this, you could respond to him with something like this:

BEHAVIOR 3: USING SALES TECHNIQUES ON YOU | 63

> *Because the price list configurations that we currently have are part of a larger company strategy, having a special one created with just list prices requires special approval. Currently our price lists show street price. Is there a reason you need one with just list prices? If so, please explain and put in the request using our standard procedure. Then, I can pass your request along to the VP of product management, who will make the decision about whether we can create this price list for you.*

Have Rules and Procedures in Place

Having rules and procedures in place for your department or even just for your own work prioritization is key to dealing with liking, friendship, exclusivity, and similarity as well as reciprocation. Because these sales techniques take advantage of the salesperson's relationship with you, the rules and procedures create a boundary that is in place despite the relationship.

- Liking, Friendship, Exclusivity, and Similarity

Prioritization rules can prevent special treatment for certain individual salespeople simply because they have formed personal relationships with individuals in your department. If your department doesn't have official rules in place, you can suggest that such a list be developed. Even without a department list, you can implement a set of prioritization rules for yourself. Examples include the following:

- All projects require a ticket and are completed in the order of receipt.

- A marketing manager must sign off on any prioritization change.

- Projects requiring graphic design require the requestor's manager's signature.

- Projects costing over $250 require management approval.

The salespeople at your company don't know your departmental policies; they won't know if the rules aren't official or if you made up your own list. Rules and procedures enable you say no without the salesperson taking it personally, and they prevent the salesperson from taking advantage of your friendship. If necessary, tell the salesperson you could get away with going around procedures once or twice, but doing it more will get you in trouble.

In addition, having policies about how requests are handled ensures fairer treatment for salespeople who are new or who don't have the opportunity to develop friendships

BEHAVIOR 3: USING SALES TECHNIQUES ON YOU | 65

in your department. Policies like this also ensure you don't waste your time thinking you have a genuine friendship with someone who may only be using a sales technique on you.

I've worked in departments that had special treatment–type rules that we only pulled out when necessary. I've never had an issue getting internal approval to put a procedure in place that's designed to make the marketing team more efficient, and you probably won't either.

- Reciprocation

Salespeople give gifts, whether tangible or intangible, because they expect something in return. The best way to deal with this technique is to avoid situations where you may feel the need to reciprocate by giving a salesperson special treatment. Don't accept invitations to lunch where a salesperson is paying. If she asks if you want a coffee drink from Starbucks, simply say, "No thanks" or pay for your own drink. If sales reps bring you gifts from trips or from clients, you can say you already have one or share it with the rest of your team. If the person tries to build you up in front of other people, give credit to the rest of your team. Of course, you can't always avoid gifts and compliments, so accept them gracefully when you must, but also be mindful of the strings that may be attached.

If you cannot avoid situations where you feel the need to reciprocate, it might help to have small items readily available so you can easily give back. For example, you can have small gifts on hand with which you can reciprocate a salesperson's generosity, rather than giving preferential treatment. Hats, T-shirts, stickers, or other giveaways that don't affect the priorities of your department are a good solution to dealing with reciprocation in a way other than preferential treatment with work projects.

Evaluate Suggestions Before Agreeing

Sales techniques like mirroring and leading, social proof, and perceived authority are designed to influence you to say yes. The best way to deal with these is to slow down and take more time to evaluate the request. Doing so can protect you from taking on more work simply because of suggestion-based sales techniques.

- Mirroring and Leading

I once worked with an extremely successful salesman who would constantly nod and say "Right?" when he was talking to people. By watching him interact with other people, I could see how well this technique generally worked for him, and I had to make a conscious effort not to respond to his "Right?" question with my own response of "Right" or "Yes, and." He was very good at getting people to do what he wanted by using this technique, even if "yes" wasn't the best response to what he was asking. I had to be hyper-aware about agreeing to anything he asked before I had time to evaluate it.

Salespeople may use mirroring so commonly that they are no longer even aware they are doing it. To combat this technique, you have to pay attention to body language, as well as the words salespeople speak. For example, you might notice a certain salesperson nods every time she speaks with you. Once you realize this, pay attention to your own body language. Your natural reaction will be to nod in response, but try to stop yourself from doing so. If you are at least aware of the mirroring and you know that it may be used to influence you, you can choose to respond (nod, say "yes," etc.) on purpose, rather than automatically.

- Social Proof

Social proof is an effective sales technique. It's easy to be influenced by the fact that a respected company is doing things a certain way. Even if the example given is from a well-respected industry leader, be sure to evaluate the request with a critical eye. Before you make any decisions, take a step back and assess the sales rep's proposal without regard to what other companies have done. Look at the potential effectiveness and consequences of implementing the suggested marketing activity. Programs that appear to be successful may not really be when you look at the costs or the results.

- Perceived Authority

When a salesperson, sales manager, or sales executive treats you as if you work for them, it's easy fall into the trap of acting as if you do. This is why your first defense against this sales technique is to recognize what is happening. Be clear in your own mind about how the salesperson is using perceived authority to influence you. Next, before you agree to any assignments from anyone in sales, evaluate how it aligns with your own priorities. Take the information, put it aside, compare it to your priorities, and if appropriate, discuss it with your manager. If you go ahead with the project from sales, report back to your own marketing management first rather than the salesperson or sales manager who gave you the "assignment."

Behavior 4

Not Reading Email

One company I worked for had a partner-sponsored promotional event at a large branch location. The marketing event manager on my team communicated information about the event to the sales managers and the sales team in multiple different ways:

- The event manager sent the branch manager and sales managers detailed information about the event far enough in advance so that they could include the topic in the branch sales meetings.

- All customers on the branch area list received three emailed invitations prior to the event, and everyone in sales was copied on the invitation each time it was sent.

- Information about the event was included twice in the weekly marketing news email that went out to the entire company.

All the event information was available on a shared calendar that the sales team was reminded to check every time they received communication from the marke ting team.

Through these multiple emails, marketing sent the sales team everything they needed to know about the event. They were told where and when it would take place, who the sponsor was, who was invited, which products were featured and detail about the promotion.

Only two salespeople showed up.

Because the event was held at a large branch location, our event manager walked around and let salespeople in the branch know that the event had started. Nearly every salesperson told her they had no idea the event was happening, that they hadn't heard anything about it, and that if they had heard about it, they definitely would have been there.

Of course, these salespeople and the sales managers had been told about the event via email multiple times well in advance and again closer to the event. They just hadn't read their email.

What It Looks Like

One of the most universal complaints about working with salespeople is that they don't read their email. Like many marketers, I've written informative, thorough, and complete email messages designed to answer all anticipated questions and ensure sales team self-sufficiency regarding a particular topic. I wrote one email that explained exactly where salespeople could find every piece of marketing collateral on their own. I wrote an email with every detail they could ever need regarding their upcoming sales meeting. I sent a thorough schedule for sales reps who would be working a trade show. However, based on the emails, calls, and texts I received afterward, it was apparent that almost none of the salespeople paid attention to the information.

Salespeople are focused on what their customers want and on what they, the sales reps, need to do in the short term to make a sale. Although it would certainly be to their advantage to read the information you send to them, the fact is that if you don't immediately get their attention and make them see that they need the information enclosed in your email, salespeople probably aren't going to read it.

Most salespeople don't really read their email; they skim it. Because of this, they often respond to detailed emails in ways that can be frustrating. Here are some examples:

- They ask a question or give a response based on the first sentence or two of your email, even if the answer and/or topic is covered in the next paragraph.

- They respond in a way that seems totally unrelated to the topic of your email or to the information you requested of them.

- They provide a short reply to give you the impression that they have read your email and are being responsive, but because they haven't read the email, you still have to spend time following up to get the information you actually requested.

It's not unusual for salespeople to write a short reply without actually having read your email. Because they want to be perceived as responsive and engaged even if they aren't, they may prioritize responding over actually reading the email. It may be immediately clear that they haven't read your email, but sometimes it isn't. Don't assume an answer means your email has actually been read.

Salespeople have learned that a quick response to customers is advantageous, and they usually reread customer emails because they may contain information that will affect their paycheck. However, this doesn't happen within the company. They most likely won't reread your emails after sending out an initial response, and thus they miss important information. Here are a few suggestions for dealing with this behavior.

How to Deal with It

The best way to deal with this behavior is to change the way you write emails. Through composition and formatting you can direct sales reps' focus to the information you are trying to communicate. By writing in a way that is designed to get salespeople's attention, you can improve the odds that they will read your email and respond the way you need them to.

Put the Request First

One marketing executive at a large software company told me, "I have two different ways I format email; one for 'normal' people, and one for salespeople. In a normal email, I typically write as if I'm telling a story with a succession of events, then the result of those events, and then finally the request I'm making of the reader. With a salesperson, I do the opposite. I put the request up front or even in the subject line, followed by the result, and then the detail underneath." This is great advice, and it ensures salespeople receive key information when skimming your email.

The topic organization of an email to a salesperson should look something like this:

- Your request, or what you need from the salesperson.

- What will be achieved based on you request, or the events leading up to and causing the request.

- Details the salesperson may need as background, or information the salesperson may need to respond or follow through with the activity.

Formatting like this takes extra effort and typically requires you to write the email first and then reorganize it so that someone who is only skimming will easily see what is required of them.

Stick to One Topic

While most people in marketing and other non-sales positions prefer and respond better to receiving one email with all the necessary information consolidated in one place, salespeople are the opposite. If there are multiple topics within one email, the salesperson may wait until he has all the answers to every item listed on your email (which may never happen) before he responds to anything at all. Even if you need to discuss a few related topics with a salesperson, you will likely get a better response if you stick to one topic or request per email. Rather than sending one long email with multiple topics, send multiple emails with one topic each. Doing so provides the salesperson the ability to focus and respond to each item separately.

Write Shorter Emails

Most salespeople aren't going to read a nine-paragraph email, or even a four-paragraph email. They might skim it or read the first one or two paragraphs, but that's about it. An outside salesperson might glance at email on her phone between client meetings. Even if she doesn't get through the whole message, it will be marked as read, and she's not going to come back and reread it.

To address this lack of attention, write shorter emails. Take out extra words and only outline information salespeople need to understand or have in order to carry out an action or give the requested response.

Here's an example of a long email versus a shortened version:

BEHAVIOR 4: NOT READING EMAIL | 75

Long:

> *Hi Sales Team!*
>
> *We paid attention to your feedback at last year's sales conference, so this year our marketing team has worked hard to deliver a new literature series that you can take advantage of and use to promote our solutions to your customers. To make it as easy as possible for you, we've formatted all items to print on letter-size paper. We've also created an easily accessible web page that you can get to anywhere, anytime, and from any device. In addition, we have professionally printed copies of the literature available for you to order on demand, along with folders and notecards.*
> *You can find all the literature online at mycompany.com/literature and you can download PDF copies directly from this website. You can also order printed copies by going to mycompany.com/intranet/orderliterature and selecting the pieces and quantities you need. We'll send the copies you order to your branch office.*
>
> *Thank you,*
> *The Marketing Director*

Short:

> *Available now! Check out the new literature you asked for at mycompany.com/literature. And, order your printed copies now at mycompany.com/intranet/orderliterature.*

Use Bullet Points

Whenever possible, avoid writing paragraphs and instead use bullet points, which are easier for salespeople to read and follow. A salesperson may not read through a paragraph, but if you change the same four-sentence paragraph into four one-sentence bullet points, he is more likely to read through all the information. For instance, this paragraph could be written as:

- Use bullets instead of paragraphs.

- Easier for the salesperson to read and follow.

- Increases likelihood he will read all info.

Use Tactical Subject Lines

Your subject line is a key way to grab salespeople's attention and draw them in to read your email. Here are some techniques for writing effective subject lines:

BEHAVIOR 4: NOT READING EMAIL | 77

- Scare tactics: Put something in the subject line to "scare" the salesperson into action. Just as an online banner headline is written to get click-throughs, your subject line should be designed to make the salesperson want to know more—specifically, how to avoid a negative consequence. Some subject line examples are "You could lose a $1M order" or "The CEO may yell at you today unless…"

- WIIFM: The "What's in it for me?" subject line is another way to entice salespeople to open and read your email. If the subject line hints that salespeople can get something they want—for example, win a contest or out-do their colleagues—they will be much more likely to read what's inside. Examples of WIIFM subject lines include "Do this to see $50k in commissions" or "You may already be winning this contest."

- The question: If you simply need an answer, ask the question in the subject line. This question may lead into the rest of the email, as in "Do you know whose account this is?" This subject line question requires the salesperson to open your email to see the name of the account and then answer either with no or with the name of the person who manages the account. Or, you may be able to include enough information for the salesperson to respond without even reading the rest of the email, as in "Is Coca-Cola your account?" This subject line doesn't require that the salesperson open the email. They have all the information they need in the subject line and can respond with yes or no without looking at the body of the email.

- Direction: You can put the task that you need the salesperson to do right in the subject line. For non-salespeople, you might write "Reports" in the subject line, and then in the body of the email say something like "If you haven't already sent me your weekly report, could you please do so by noon today? I need it for my meeting at that time." For salespeople, however, you could put the direction right in the subject line—"Send weekly report before NOON TODAY"—knowing the body of the email probably won't be read.

- The whole email: Another tactic is to write the whole email in your subject line. I know this tactic works with salespeople because they use it with each other and with marketing people. I've received email from salespeople with three-line subjects and nothing in the body. Although other professionals in your office might find this email style abrupt, salespeople seem to respond well to having all the necessary info in the subject line. An example of this tactic would be something like "When is Japan trip & is Kevin going? Pls take samples: ready on Wed."

Emphasize Key Words and Use Formatting Strategically

To make sure the salesperson sees the important part

BEHAVIOR 4: NOT READING EMAIL | 79

of your email, use boldface, italics, underlining, different colors, highlighting, or all caps to emphasize the key points. You might change the formatting on two or three key words or a whole sentence—whatever you want to ensure the salesperson sees, even if he only skims your email.

Here's an example of an email formatted for a salesperson:

Subject: PLEASE RESPOND: Inventory at risk for UAINC

Hi James,

When do you expect the P.O. from Umbrella Awnings Inc?

If I don't hear back from you by COB THURSDAY, *I will not be able to hold inventory allocation* for you for this order.

Because you mentioned the potential order last week, I wanted to warn you that:
- Inventory is limited until next quarter, and the ORDER MUST BE CONFIRMED by the end of the week.
- IF YOU DON'T CONFIRM the order, new order shipments won't be received until *November.*

Set Flags and Reminders

If you need a reply or if you need to verify the salesperson understood what you wrote, you must follow up. The easiest way to do this is with electronic reminders. One example is an email flag with a deadline that pops up prior to the time you need a response. If you'd like to get this flag reminder as well, you can list yourself as a recipient or set one for yourself at the same time you set the recipient reminder. Another way to set an electronic reminder is by creating a task or a calendar event with a note that the task must be completed. For example, you can invite the salesperson to a meeting on Thursday with the subject "Provide PO information before 3pm." You don't need to have a meeting, and the salesperson may call you in confusion wondering what you are having the meeting about. This is fine, since you got her attention with the reminder, which was your objective.

If Necessary, Copy the Boss

Sometimes salespeople won't pay attention until you copy their manager, VP, or depending on the size of your company, the CEO. There is at least one person in your organization each salesperson is concerned about impressing. If you have tried the other tactics and the salesperson still doesn't read emails or provide the requested information, your best bet may be to copy that higher-up person on very important emails. I can guarantee that you are not the first person to do this, and the person's boss is probably used to it. Copying the manager risks compromising the trust level with a coworker in sales, but if you are at the end of your rope and are more worried about getting a response than how the salesperson feels about it, this is a tactic you may need to use.

Behavior 5

Not Listening

Once, when I was a product manager, I held an internal training for a small group of salespeople who sold a certain type of services for our company. The options and pricing had changed due to a new contract with our supplier, and I wanted to help the salespeople understand the changes. Only eight salespeople were required to attend and they were dispersed across the country, so I held the training online. The training was short, simple, and straightforward and it was only for their benefit; I wasn't asking them to do anything. Within a few days, each salesperson who attended the online training called to ask me about the changes they had just noticed in the services options and pricing. Even though my online training had been done for their benefit, it was apparent that none of them had actually listened.

What It Looks Like

Have you ever explained something to a salesperson in what you thought was a clear and concise way, only to have the person come back to you later as if the conversation, explanation, or training never happened? Salespeople of all levels are notorious for not listening, even when it comes to information designed to benefit them and make their job easier.

Perhaps you've had an experience like this: A salesperson is trying to explain to a customer how investing in good equipment will save them money in the long run. During the course of the conversation, the salesperson says she wishes she had an easy way to calculate this for the customer, a sales tool that shows total cost of ownership (TCO). After the phone call with the customer, the salesperson contacts you to suggest that you have a TCO tool created—not remembering that you created a TCO calculator tool last year, that it is already live on the website, and that you gave a demonstration of the tool at the last sales meeting. Or, a salesperson may suggest that you produce a how-to video on a topic to which you have already dedicated an entire series on your company's YouTube channel. Or, he may request to have literature created that already exists, suggest a promotion you just had, or any number of similar ideas that may make you feel like no one is listening or paying attention.

At one company, a VP of sales copied me on a series of email exchanges with an outside sales rep who was asking to have materials created about our company's services. I responded to the exchange, redirecting the salesperson and the VP to the easily accessible materials that already existed a shared cloud drive that could be accessed from anywhere or with any device by all of our company's salespeople. I mentioned that I had recently presented these materials to the sales team and had demonstrated how to access them more than once.

The sales VP sent me a note after the exchange that said, "Point here—no one listens or uses the tools—frustrating."

I responded, "I know. It's nothing new. It's the same everywhere, I'm just resolved to consistent repetition and redirection to easily accessible tools :-)"

He responded with "Yes, EVERWHERE this happens! A.D.D. salespeople!"

I had to laugh because the sales VP was as guilty of this as anyone, but it was still satisfying to have him acknowledge that not listening is a consistent issue with salespeople. It is a universal truth that you'll have to tell salespeople the same information multiple times.

How to Deal with It

Salespeople not listening is a common problem and it can lead to other problems, like not completing projects or not understanding and following directions and priorities. Salespeople often prioritize communication from their customers and treat everything else as if it's background noise, the result being that they just don't listen to your communication to them. While you may not be able to actually make them listen, you can have strategies to deal with the results of them not listening. If you're like me, you don't have time to give everyone on the sales team individual attention. To increase the odds of getting sales to listen, design your communication to grab their attention and make it almost impossible for them to not follow directions.

Idiot-Proof Your Processes

One way to deal with salespeople who don't listen is to make processes exceedingly simple. Idiot-proofing procedures is especially helpful if you're working with a large sales team and you don't have the time to give any special attention, to interpret meaning, or to correct mistakes. The key is to make request and response options so regimented that it's impossible for salespeople to do it wrong. Idiot-proofing involves creating documents with drop-down menus and limited choices, as well as locking documents so that they can't be edited. It requires more work up front, but it's worth the effort in the long run.

One way to idiot-proof something is to route the salesperson through a process where she needs to check what is already available before making a new request. For instance, I worked at a company where our online request for new literature routed the salesperson to look at currently available literature by category before requesting anything new. This process ensured that the salesperson would find what she needed if it existed already and would not ask for something that duplicated effort that had already been made.

Another idiot-proofing technique is to have salespeople use a request form that cannot be submitted until it is 100 percent complete. This ensures that you have all the information you need before starting a project, so you won't have to go back and ask for more details. For instance, if a salesperson is requesting that you participate in a trade show, your form may ask who the audience is, the reason for the show, the cost, the location, what type of support is needed, and the dates of the event, in addition to other key dates or deadlines. This may make it harder for the salesperson to submit the request, but it will be more efficient for you once you receive it because you won't have to go back and ask for missing information.

Although idiot-proofing ensures things get done the right way, it's not always necessary or even the best option. This technique requires extra thought, time, and resources on your part, so it's probably not the best use of your energy to treat every situation this way. In addition, providing material in a regimented way limits input that can sometimes be valuable. But, if you don't want to explain the same thing multiple times or ask the same questions over and over, or if you want to ensure that you have all the information you need up front, you can structure documents, requests, and other materials in a careful and leading way so that no information is missed, even if people don't listen.

Give Personal Attention

Using personal attention to deal with salespeople who don't listen should be used as a last resort. It's impossible to give this attention to every salesperson, and if you're like me, it's hard to find an extra hour to sit with someone and walk them through a process that they should be able to get through on their own. Sometimes, however, if you need to get something finished, giving personal attention to some salespeople is your only option.

When I needed to get customer intelligence data from a salesperson and I couldn't get him to respond with the right information, I ended up giving him personal attention so that I could finish my project. I scheduled time with the sales rep and we talked through the information about each one of his target accounts until we had them all categorized. Then, I made the updates to the data myself. It took me at least as much time to walk him through the process than it would have taken for him to do it alone, probably more. It wasn't the easiest solution or one that I would recommend unless personal attention is the only way to finish your project.

Provide Information Access

In the course of your job, you provide marketing-related instructions to salespeople. However, if the sales reps don't need the information at that exact moment, they most likely won't retain what you've said. When they do encounter a situation where they need the marketing-related information you already provided, they won't remember it and will call you. To avoid spending time helping each salesperson individually, you should make it extremely easy for salespeople to access all marketing materials and related instructions. Accessing marketing materials should be no more difficult than sending or receiving an email, and procedures should be obvious even if there has been little or no training.

Because salespeople are often out in the field, they need quick access to information about programs and products. An ideal way to provide this is with a cloud drive, like Google Drive or Dropbox, rather than a shared drive on your company network. You can even put all the materials on a web page, with or without a password, depending on the level of confidentiality. Salespeople should be able to get to the items they need using any device, including their company or personal mobile phone, tablet, a computer at a client site, or even a print shop copier. Forcing salespeople to log on to your company's VPN to download materials will only lead to them contacting you for help, which will make you less efficient while increasing your workload.

Yes, salespeople should listen the first time you give them information, but they won't. If you put information and materials on a shared drive or web page, you can simply point the sales team to the accessible location of the files every time you receive a request for previously provided information that is stored there. As much as possible, always respond to requests with the same basic information, for instance, "This item can always be found on our team drive at https://drive.google.com/xxxx," or "We already have an item that fits this description available for download at [yourcompanywebsite].com/literature/."

This type of consistent response trains your organization's sales team to look on your shared drive or web page first, before contacting you. It also gives you the chance to show the sales team that the marketing team has thought about their needs and has provided sales with relevant materials, and that salespeople already have easy access to what they need from marketing. Should a salesperson ever use the fact that you or your team were unavailable or unresponsive as an excuse for not having the materials they need, it will be clear to everyone, especially your management, that the salesperson should have first looked on the easily accessible site for the information.

Behavior 6
Nagging

I worked with a senior salesperson who was responsible for an important segment of the company's business. Shortly after I started as the company's marketing manager, she expressed that she needed me to create a line card listing all of the partners and suppliers she worked with that were applicable to her business. She wanted the card available online and in print so she could hand it out when she visited customers and when she attended industry events.

For me, creating this card was very simple; I just needed the salesperson to give me a list of her partners before I could have the layout and printing done. I even had an in-person meeting with the sales rep to go over what I needed. During the meeting, the rep decided that rather than coming up with a list at that moment, she would peruse some old materials and use them to help her complete the list after our meeting.

She didn't respond for weeks, and I found myself nagging her about it for a while. I finally stopped because it really didn't make a difference to me or the rest of the sales

BEHAVIOR 6: NAGGING | 89

team if the line card was done; it only made a difference to her. Since she didn't provide input, I put the job aside.

A couple of weeks later, the sales rep contacted me in a panic. She had an event the next day and asked if I had her line card ready. I took a deep breath and responded that I did not have it ready because I had not received her input. I told her I would be happy to rush it through same day if she would send me the information now. She didn't send the information. I sent her a line card template that she could edit and put in the information herself. I told her she could fill it in while traveling since I couldn't get it done ahead of time without the information, and I asked her to send me a copy when she was done. She didn't do this either.

A month later she had a last-minute request for another event and the same thing happened. It became a crazy circle of her nagging me about needing the line card and me nagging her back about needing the information with which to create the line card.

Finally, I realized that it was never going to work, and I found a way around the problem. By working with one of our company's purchasing managers, I put together a list of the suppliers whose products the salesperson typically sold to her customers. I prepared the line card based on this information and formatted it so she could use it as needed and easily edit out the few suppliers she wasn't actively working with and add in the ones that I had missed.

What It Looks Like

Nagging falls into two categories:
1. The nagging salesperson
2. The salesperson who needs nagging

The story at the beginning of this chapter falls into both categories but mostly the second—the salesperson who needs nagging. While the salesperson would nag me periodically about the piece of literature she needed, I had to nag her to get the information to get it done.

Whether you're on the giving or receiving end, nagging is annoying and frustrating. Nagging can also be a pervasive behavior when working with salespeople, so it's wise to have a strategy in place to deal with problem.

The Nagging Salesperson

When salespeople ask you for something over and over, even if it's out of your hands, they're nagging. For instance, they may repeatedly ask you for the status of their project—even if you've responded to them previously and communicated specifics about when it will be completed. If you're in creative services or another group that has a queue of projects, you probably deal with this issue often.

When you have a salesperson's project in a queue, even if it has an assigned priority level and timeline, the nagging salesperson will keep checking on the status even though the project deadline hasn't passed. Sometimes this nagging behavior works and the salesperson receives his project ahead of schedule, but only because the marketer wants to get the nagging salesperson out of their hair. However, giving in to the salesperson only reinforces the behavior and increases their tendency to nag you and your team more in the future.

One sales VP I worked with consistently asked me to do things three or four times. Despite my acknowledging the request the first time and the fact that the project might take a month, the VP would ask me three times in the first couple days after his initial request. At one point I stopped him and pointed out that he was asking me to do the same thing multiple times—sometimes literally within minutes of the previous request. That is, he was nagging. I let him know in a nice and humorous way that he didn't need to make multiple requests, that I understood the information per my response the first time, and that he should give me at least enough time in between requests to let me work on the project.

This VP acknowledged what he was doing. He explained that he asked me to do the same thing multiple times because he was used to dealing with salespeople who typically required multiple requests and reminders before they took action. This was an eye-opening insight into salesperson behavior. Because of his years of experience managing salespeople who need nagging, the VP was unnecessarily nagging me, which was extremely annoying and may have even resulted in the opposite of what he wanted. My natural response to being nagged is to set clear boundaries and timelines and limit communication about a project until the deadline is reached. I've confirmed with other non-sales professionals that they sometimes send the requests of nagging salespeople to the bottom of the pile.

Salespeople Who Need Nagging

The sales VP I confronted about his nagging was doing so because he was used to nagging the salespeople who reported to him. As an experienced sales manager he had made nagging part of his regular routine to ensure productivity. He did it to make sure that the salespeople had heard him, knew he was serious, and would take action. If there's anyone that salespeople should be responding to without nagging, it's their team vice president! In most instances, this VP was their boss's boss. Even so, he found it necessary to follow up three times as part of his standard procedure when working with salespeople. This shows that marketers aren't the only ones who need to nag salespeople to meet our objectives. In other words, it's not us; it's them.

The fact is that some salespeople won't respond or complete actions items unless you keep following up with them. This gets tiresome. It is also an uncomfortable task for those of us who find it extremely annoying when someone nags us in the same way. The unfortunate fact is that if you only communicate your requirements to a salesperson once, she may not see it, or she may assume it's not that important since you didn't continue to press her for a response. Because the need to be nagged is typical behavior for many salespeople and because many salespeople are used to receiving multiple requests for the same thing, you will probably need to do some nagging if you need a result.

How to Deal with It

Whether you have to work with someone who asks you about her project status multiple times or whether you need to repeatedly ask the salesperson for input, nagging can lead to built-up frustration. Having a plan to deal with nagging can help you preserve your sanity and push projects forward when they stall because of someone who isn't responding.

The Nagging Salesperson

No matter what measures you take to deal with this behavior, you will likely have some salespeople who will continue to nag you until a project is done. Still, with strategies in place, you can avoid the frustration and wasted time they cause.

- Respond with Clear Notification

When salespeople make a request, give them clear notification via email or other automated response that you received their communication. It's best that you do this in writing so that if there is ever a question about project status, timeline, or what was expected, you have documentation. Notification via email could be something as simple as this:

> *Thank you for your request. I'll review the information and get back to you with any questions in the next couple days.*

Because it is time-samped, an email response gives you a record of the project start time even if the original request was verbal. In addition, the salesperson knows that you received her request and that you will respond. Knowing the next step might alleviate the salesperson's need to follow up with you right away to check on the status.

- Require a Form or Ticket

This technique helps to keep some departments, such as creative services, organized. It also provides reassurance to the salesperson that their request will get attention because with a ticket, the salesperson should get some notification that their request has been received and is in a queue for action and response.

There are different ways to implement a form or ticket procedure. The low-tech way is to have salespeople make a project request by filling out a simple form and returning it. The form could be a PDF or Word document that's emailed or a hard copy that's filled out in person and submitted (you could then scan it to have a digital copy). You'll have to train people to use the form by asking them to fill it in when they make a request.

The higher-tech and somewhat more elegant way to implement this strategy is to have an online or email-based ticketing system. This type of system auto-generates a ticket when the salesperson makes a request via an online form or when requests are sent to a designated email address. Your company might already have this kind of system in place for employee help requests from the IT department. If so, people in your company—including salespeople—have likely already

BEHAVIOR 6: NAGGING

used it when they need help from IT, so it will not be a big leap to get them to start using it for marketing requests.

If you have even a small marketing group and you have a sizable sales team with people who send multiple requests, I highly recommend investing in an automated ticketing system. It has advantages beyond just putting projects into a funnel. It allows you and your team to fairly prioritize requests, keep track of projects, and quantify the number of projects that are completed. It may also give you visibility to which people are managing different projects and how much time is spent on each one. This information enables you to give management metrics about your work and your team's productivity. If you're so inspired, it's also a great way to prove to your management that you are just as productive working remotely as you are working in the office because you'll be able to show the number of tickets you clear working at home is the same as or more than the number of tickets you clear when working in the office.

Setting up ticketing, or even a simple form procedure, will initially require some extra effort for you and your team. You'll need to choose a system, understand how to use it, and create the associated documents, including the form content and auto-response email. Depending on what method you use, there may or may not be a cost involved. After the system is set up, you will need to communicate the new procedure to your organization and do some simple training.

Like many things, use of a ticketing system, whether high tech or low tech, often follows an 80/20 rule: about 80 percent of the people will follow the procedure and 20 percent will continue to go around it. It's your choice as to how far you push the requirement. Based on the experience I've had with this type of system, you'll need to have ongoing communication with sales about using it because some people will continue to contact you directly every time they want your help. When they do, make sure your response includes information about submitting a ticket. You could also say that you will submit the ticket for them this time, with an explanation of how they can do it themselves next time. You should also explain that the ticket is necessary and important for you to have. Here's an example of an email explaining this:

> *Hi Jerry,*
>
> *Thank you for contacting me regarding your customer event.*
>
> *I am opening a marketing ticket for you for this request. It will be routed to the event manager in your region, who will follow up with you. In the future, to have your request expedited, you can open a ticket simply by emailing your request to marketingticket@ourcompany.com. By doing this, your request will be routed to the correct person faster, and a ticket will automatically be created.*
>
> *Cheers,*
>
> *Tasha*

BEHAVIOR 6: NAGGING | 97

You should thoughtfully consider whether you are ready to implement a ticket system before you do it. I don't recommend starting and stopping; once you stop, it will be a challenge to re-implement the procedure.

- Set a Timeline

Another technique to curb nagging is giving the salesperson a timeline, in addition to confirmation that the request was received. If it's an informal request, you can simply send them an email like this:

> *Per our conversation today, you are requesting development of a TCO analysis tool, and I'll have a first draft of it back to you by COB Monday 8/13.*

If the salesperson has submitted a formal request on a form, you can have an automated response ready to go that says something like this:

> *Thank you for your creative services request. Your request is in our queue and someone from our team will contact you in the next 4 business days with any questions. In general, depending on size and complexity, projects take 8–10 business days.*

- Provide an Automated Response

If salespeople nag you about project status before the project deadline has passed, provide an automated response to their email. This response might be a literal automatic reply or it might be a standard reply that works for almost everyone and all circumstances.

If you have a separate email address for incoming projects and project communication, your automatic reply may be something like this:

> *Thank you for your email. If this is a new project, please ensure you have provided all necessary materials and we will respond back to you with a project deadline date. If this email is regarding a current project that has not yet reached the deadline date, please note that we will communicate back to you by the specified project deadline.*

If you don't have a separate project email, you can write a standard response ahead of time and copy and paste it as needed. A copy-and-paste response could look something like this:

BEHAVIOR 6: NAGGING | 99

> *Thank you for your email requesting creative services. We will review your request within one business day and respond with any questions. Creative projects typically take eight business days but times vary depending on your project and other pending requests.*

This will save you the effort of having to write something new each time. If you work with a large sales team, unique individual responses waste a lot of time and accomplish little. Prewritten responses to standard inquiries will help make you be more efficient and will send a message to salespeople that you aren't going to give individual updates prior to specified deadlines.

- Stick to the Exact Deadline

It goes without saying that you should give yourself enough time when agreeing to deadlines, and you should get requested projects done before deadlines pass. What I'm cautioning against here is delivering the completed project too early. If an activity normally takes you seven days and you have a particularly slow week and manage to finish in one day, the next time that salesperson needs something from you, she may default to telling you it must be done in one day. Because you were previously able to complete a project in one day, one day will be the salesperson's new frame of reference for how long projects really take. She will believe that you can and will get it done for her since you did it before.

Getting projects done early and off your plate early may be nice for you, but it trains the salespeople at your organization to expect you to work within tighter deadlines, and nagging may result if you don't meet those expectations. Although you may have finished projects ready to deliver, resist the urge to return projects too early, and instead put them aside for delivery on or just before the agreed-upon deadline.

- Confront if Necessary

As I had to do with the sales VP who asked me for everything at least three times, sometimes you just need to tactfully let the salesperson, sales manager, or sales VP know that you heard them and that you don't need nagging. They might not even realize what they are doing, so you might be doing them, and the rest of the people you work with, a favor.

If you need to confront someone about nagging, be sure to do it diplomatically and at the right time. You may even try to make it humorous. Remember, it's important for you to maintain a good relationship with sales and sales management, so say it in such a way that doesn't make enemies.

Salespeople Who Need Nagging

With salespeople who need nagging to fulfill requests, your goal isn't to bug them less; your goal is to make nagging them less annoying and cumbersome for you.

- Provide Clear Communication

One way to decrease your need to nag is to provide clear communication. Tell salespeople exactly what you need done, how they should do it, and by when. Provide well-defined parameters, specific instructions, and precise timelines. Put the information in writing so that you have a record of it.

For example, if you need a team of salespeople to categorize a list of their accounts, you could provide them with the following:

- A list of their accounts in a format they can easily access and edit
- A list of categories they should use and definitions of those categories, formatted in a drop-down menu or another finite idiot-proof list
- A specific date and time by which you need the work completed

If you make a request verbally, even if it is small, always follow it up with a written request via email. Then you will have documented communication to forward to them if they "forget" the request was made at all. By making sure that verbal communication is backed up in writing with an email, you will also cover yourself should you have any issues with your own deadlines because of a salesperson's lack of response.

- Provide Graduated Deadlines

Another way to decrease nagging on your part is to provide graduated deadlines in the original request. To do this take your request and break it down into multiple parts and give each of those parts a deadline.

For example, in your request for account categorization, you could give graduated deadlines such as the following:

- January 10, 5:00 p.m.: Provide/confirm your list of all accounts for categorization
- January 15, 5:00 p.m.: Provide a list of any accounts that should be excluded from corporate communication
- January 20, 5:00 p.m.: Provide your final list of enterprise customers
- January 25, 5:00 p.m.: Provide your final list of SMB customers

Looking at this list, a smart sales rep might realize it will take less time to do the work in one sitting and get the whole thing to you by January 10. For the salesperson who tends to procrastinate, this breakdown of deadlines will provide them with smaller, more manageable tasks. It will also give you a chance to legitimately, and even automatically, follow up after each deadline without having to nag.

- Automate Emails and Reminders

Automated emails and reminders allow you to follow up without driving yourself crazy with reminders at each deadline or interval. For instance, you can use automated email to follow up on the previous graduated deadline list. Email programs such as Microsoft Outlook have a feature where you can write an email in advance and schedule it to go out at a predetermined time. If you take the time in advance to write a series of reminders and schedule the reminder emails to go out at the scheduled deadlines, you don't even need to think about nagging the sales reps until you come close to the final deadline.

At the beginning of any prescheduled email, put a note up front for salespeople who have already done the work, or they may bother you each time you send an automated email to confirm that you already received the information. Here's an example of an automated email reminding salespeople of a deadline:

> *If you have already provided the information requested, THANK YOU, and please ignore this email.*
>
> *If you haven't yet done so, this is a reminder that your categorized list of enterprise customers is due back to marketing@company.com by 5:00 p.m. PST today, January 20.*

If you don't want to send out automated emails, you can also attach a reminder flag to the original email, create task reminders, or send out calendar items that will pop up and remind the salesperson to do the work at the scheduled time. As a rule, whenever possible, use automation. While it may seem like a hassle up front, automated emails will save you time in the longer term. You won't have to spend time personally interfacing with the sales team so you can focus on your own productivity and your own priorities.

Behavior 7
Oversimplifying

I worked with a salesperson who needed large posters of a map showing the logos of each of the partners she was working with in the correct location on the map. With her request she sent an image that she had put together using PowerPoint. It looked good; it had the map in the background and each of the logos in the right place. However, she didn't understand that I couldn't just send the PowerPoint to a printer and have posters made. Because of the required image resolution for printing posters, the artwork had to be re-done, and I needed vector images of all the affiliate company logos for the designer. The salesperson oversimplified the project, and she expected me to have her posters done in a day or two. In actuality, the project involved getting the logos we didn't already have from several organizations, having the artwork done by a graphic designer, and then sending the file to a printer. It ultimately took about three weeks to complete the project, versus the couple days the salesperson originally assumed it would take.

What It Looks Like

Oversimplification involves incorrectly assuming that the requested job is easier than it really is. When salespeople oversimplify, they assume that the request is simple and that it should be done quickly. They have no concept of the analysis, planning, process, detailed work, time, or requirements that may go in to accomplishing the requested marketing activity.

Because salespeople oversimplify, when you give them a realistic deadline and cost for a project, they may become frustrated, go rogue, and even start bad-mouthing you. Their perception is that you are slow and are making things more difficult than they should be. It's to your advantage to anticipate oversimplification by salespeople and prevent it from causing problems for you and for your department.

How to Deal with It

When your projects are more complex than people outside your department realize, you may have an issue with the way people perceive the amount of work you are accomplishing. Dealing with oversimplification the right way will increase the respect people have for the complexity of your work and may help you obtain additional resources you need.

Show Your Process

In some instances, you can invite salespeople into your world to give them some understanding of the complexity of what you do and the decision-making processes you go through in marketing. This can be done fairly easily. For

BEHAVIOR 7: OVERSIMPLIFYING | 107

example, you might have a salesperson sit with you while you review or create a document, or you might invite her to attend a conference call or meeting where project issues are discussed.

Inviting a salesperson to a meeting for the development of a marketing requirements document (MRD) or a similarly complex project can be very eye-opening. Getting the salesperson to actually participate can be challenging. To encourage participation, tell the salesperson you need his input. You might even ask the manager to approve the sales rep's attendance, which will increase the likelihood the salesperson will show up. Attending one or two of these meetings will shift salespeople's perception, and they will likely take you at your word next time you explain that a project is deceivingly complicated and will take more time than they expect. After salespeople see up close what is involved in developing and executing marketing plans and programs, they will generally let you handle all the details in the future. They will also have more understanding and patience when it comes to your process and time frame for completing marketing projects.

In the first section of this book I relayed a story about some salespeople who wore black in protest of my presentation about a new marketing strategy and campaign. At the end of my presentation they asked questions that indicated they assumed the new messaging had been put together arbitrarily. In reality, I had worked with some very smart people from the company's well-known agency to research messages that would resonate with our key buyers and drive the types of customer behavior we wanted. All of the new messaging we developed had been carefully tested in surveys and focus groups. The salespeople somehow thought I just came up with ideas and went with them, without regard for how our customers would react. They had no idea how much research, analysis, and testing went into developing our new campaign.

Because my company conducted focus groups at trade shows where both customers and salespeople were in attendance, I invited three salespeople from that office to sit in and watch focus groups at the next conference. None of the salespeople had observed a focus group before, and they were surprised at the detailed process involved in customer research as we developed products, messaging, and campaigns.

Since my experience with the sales rep protest, I've made it a standard practice to use salespeople as part of any research for developing new materials, including messaging, products, or programs. I regularly schedule focus groups with salespeople to take advantage of their insights about customer behavior. Getting them to be part of the research process gives me insight into their experiences with customers and feedback they have received from their clients. It gets the salespeople invested in my outcome, which in part results from their participation. Including salespeople also gets them on my side, as they are much more likely to actively support any campaign they were involved in creating.

Explain Potential Consequences

Another way to address oversimplification is to explain the worst-case-scenario consequences of taking shortcuts. In all likelihood salespeople have not considered what other projects and activities could be affected, what could go wrong by taking shortcuts, or what will be excluded from the result. Explaining the downfalls of doing a project the wrong way will help salespeople appreciate why you are taking the time to do it right and how that benefits them.

Here are some examples of worst-case-scenario consequences:

- If we don't run even a small change in wording through our standard compliance process, we could risk the company's FDA compliance, and in the event of an audit, we would put the product, the company, and our jobs at risk.

- If we run the campaign the way you are suggesting, we will cannibalize a different, successful campaign, which we would then have to cancel, and the leads you are receiving from that campaign would go away.

- If I have the poster printed from a file that is low resolution, it will look fuzzy and you won't be able to use it, but we will still need to pay for the printing.

- If we don't have the partner logos and taglines preapproved, we could lose tens of thousands of dollars in partner marketing funds, and we would have to cut other programs, such as the trade show you just requested that we participate in.

I worked for a large computer company that relied on partner marketing funding—millions of dollars—from a large semiconductor company. Because much of the business-to-business marketing activity took place in the field, sales organizations were given branding guidelines for how marketing and advertising activity should incorporate the partner logo and what proof of performance should be returned to justify the funding. For instance, the partner logo had to be a certain size and used in a certain way. We also had to get the usage preapproved and take photos to confirm that we executed the activity correctly. Getting salespeople to comply with these requirements was challenging, but the justification for the funds could usually be shoehorned through anyway.

On one occasion, however, the partner company chose to hold my company to very strict compliance, and an audit was done about a year after the marketing funds had already been received. The partner went through the submissions with a fine-tooth comb. If a banner had been set up improperly, it wasn't accepted. If the pictures weren't good enough, they weren't accepted. Because branding guidelines were not always followed to the letter in the field and because proof of

BEHAVIOR 7: OVERSIMPLIFYING | 111

performance was not always gathered per the guidelines, my company had to actually pay back nearly a million dollars in marketing funds that had been spent the previous year.

I didn't work there when the funds had been spent, but I did work there when we had to return the funds. This worst-case-scenario situation was, honestly, awful. It could have been avoided by not oversimplifying the process involved with partner branding and claiming of partner marketing funds. If my company had taken time to explain the complexity of process and the potential consequences to the people working in the field, we could have passed the audit and kept the funds.

Showing salespeople your processes and explaining what you are doing and why will help you to avoid issues like this. It will also give the sales team more respect for you and your job because they have more visibility into how much you need to accomplish to have your programs be successful.

Behavior 8

Talking Too Much

When I was a marketing manager at one company, I was on a call with my boss (the company's marketing director) and one of our company's newly appointed sales VPs. The VP had been at the company for some time and was taking over sales for a particular segment of customer. The call was about his vision for what marketing materials should be developed for his assigned customer segment. It was also an opportunity for him to offer insight and guidance to help us create the additional materials he needed to help his sales team be successful.

During the call, the sales VP dominated the conversation, explaining the materials he wanted to have created rather than taking the time to learn what we had already developed. Within a few minutes, it became clear that we had already created much of what he was asking for—he just hadn't reviewed the existing marketing materials. In his mind, everything he was asking for was his new, original idea. It didn't occur to him that we might have already had the same ideas and created materials to support the sales team. Also, some of the sales

BEHAVIOR 8: TALKING TOO MUCH | 113

VP's requests were impractical and would necessitate things like constant literature updates and customization.

To my director's credit, he didn't pipe up and let the sales VP know that most of what he was asking for was already created and that the rest should be done a different way. Instead, he listened and let the VP dominate the conversation. He masterfully agreed with all the VP's suggestions and asked a few leading questions to get the VP to think differently about the parts that were impractical (like putting people's photos on printed literature, meaning the literature would have to be updated every time we had a personnel change). In the end, the VP felt great about himself and about working with me and my director on marketing materials, he perceived that we were doing exactly what he had asked for, and we actually came away with very little work to do.

Most salespeople love to talk. Although dealing with a salesperson or executive who talks to much can be annoying, you may have the opportunity to use this behavior to your advantage the way my director did. Alternatively, you may also need to have a strategy in place to be heard when the person you're dealing with won't stop talking.

What It Looks Like

Salespeople talking too much can take different forms, from not letting you get a word in edgewise to saying more than they should. Some salespeople have also trained themselves to be good listeners, but many salespeople simply love to talk, and they love to share information with their customers and colleagues. Understanding this tendency and being prepared to deal with it can save you a lot of time and at least a few headaches.

Too Much Actual Talking

Have you ever been on a conference call with two sales VPs? I was the marketing director for a company where I occasionally needed to have a call with both our VP of sales for the west and our VP of sales for the east. The first time I had one of these calls, I found that I could hardly get a word in edgewise. Instead of addressing specific topics on our agenda, they would come up with new ideas, repeat what the other one had said, feed off each other, get excited about topics and go off on tangents, and repeat themselves multiple times. It was exhausting.

This is a common issue not only with sales VPs but with salespeople in general. When you're on a call or in a meeting with a group of salespeople, they typically talk over one another so that it's hard for you to get a chance to speak. Unless they are held to a tight agenda, they may change the discussion to something entirely different than the original purpose for the meeting. You may have found that salespeople get excited about an idea you introduce, talk about it, and then repeat it as if it's their idea.

Saying Too Much

In addition to talking too much, sales professionals often say too much. They reveal programs before they are released, talk about products that aren't out, and cause

BEHAVIOR 8: TALKING TOO MUCH | 115

disruption by giving their customers the inside scoop on upcoming price and discount changes before marketing is ready for them to hear about it.

A product manager at a large, prominent manufacturer told me a story about salespeople saying too much. The manager and her team met internally with a group of salespeople to get feedback on some preliminary product ideas. None of the products had been developed, and the discussion was not represented to be any more than an idea feedback session. After the meeting, a salesperson who had attended went on a call with a big, key customer and sold one of the undeveloped product ideas. Because the customer was so important, the company didn't want to go back and tell them that the product hadn't even been developed. The product team had to race to develop a viable product based on the idea that the salesperson had presented and sold to the customer.

Be very careful about discussing confidential or pre-release information—not-yet-released product information, company financial information, channel program changes, pricing changes, and so on—with anyone in sales, even sales VPs. Once you share information with a salesperson or anyone in the sales organization, it's as if you have leaked that information to the public. The salesperson may use whatever information you gave them to gain favor with their customer by giving them the "inside scoop," even if you have been adamant about the fact that the information is not final and is extremely confidential.

How to Deal with It

There was a time when people thought I was shy. The fact is, I was just too polite. Rather than assume a leadership position, I would defer to others if they seemed to want it, and I wouldn't make sure my ideas got through, even if I thought they were better. This didn't help my career. In order to be perceived as a person of any authority at your organization, you need to be heard. If you're especially polite, learning to deal with people who talk too much takes boldness and practice, but it's worth the effort.

Interrupt

I'm naturally a person who waits for a break in the conversation before opening my mouth to speak in a meeting. After years of working with salespeople and sales managers, however, I've had to change. I'm no longer afraid to interrupt them during a meeting or a call. Because salespeople tend to talk over one another, if I refrain from interrupting, I won't be able to get my input across and accomplish my objectives. If you're like me, you need to learn to interrupt the conversation when you are working with salespeople who are talking too much.

Be the Leader

Another way to deal with talkative salespeople is to take the position of authority at the beginning of meetings. This will be easy if you have included an objective with the meeting notification or if you prepare an agenda. You can do this with a small amount of preparation, even if it's not your meeting. If possible, speak up first and review the objective.

This will put you squarely in a leadership position. Once you have established that you have authority, you'll be able to stop salespeople from talking too much when they go off on tangents. Remind them of the meeting objective and bring the topic back to the agenda.

Have an Agenda

Although preparing an agenda can be a hassle, you need one if you're having any kind of a meeting, in person or on the phone, that includes anyone from the sales organization. The agenda doesn't need to be extensive. It can consist of three or four bullets in the copy of the invitation or in an email sent out in advance. Review the agenda at the beginning of the meeting, and when the discussion veers off topic, bring it back to the written agenda. Even if it's not your meeting, spend a few minutes ahead of time to write out notes with an agenda; if an agenda already exists, create notes related to it. Preparing notes will give you a reason to speak up at the beginning of a meeting that you didn't call. If you don't, the salesperson, sales manager, or sales VP will be more aggressive and talkative, and the meeting will likely take longer and not be as productive.

Be Clear

To deal with salespeople who say too much, you need to be clear when you share confidential information that it is indeed confidential. You should also confirm the confidentiality in writing to cover yourself. One of the best ways to do this is to send a brief email following any conversation regarding confidential information. The email is useful to recap the call anyway, and it doesn't need to be overly detailed or extensive. Usually, a few sentences are sufficient:

> *Thanks for taking the time today to discuss product features for the FC811. Per our conversation, I'll take the suggestions from the meeting back to product marketing for consideration. Please note that discussions regarding the new product are confidential and should not be discussed at this time with any customer or channel partner, even those under NDA.*

An email like this should remind salespeople to treat the subject as confidential. If they still share the information, you have at least covered yourself in writing.

Behavior 9
Sandbagging and Exaggerating

When I was a product manager for a company that manufactured overseas, the process of forecasting correctly was critical. Once products were ordered from the factory based on my team's forecasts, it would take months for products to be manufactured, shipped, and into the hands of customers. If sales exceeded our forecast, we experienced product shortages and the product would go on allocation, meaning customers with the most critical need would receive the product first, and other customers would have to wait until we had more product in stock. My product team depended on information from sales for our forecasts and to ensure that we had the product on hand to accommodate large business deals.

Everything was going along as planned, until a key customer placed a large unforecasted order, which then caused product shortages and created a ripple effect that ultimately cost the company a huge amount of money in lost margins and caused increased effort and anxiety for me and the rest of my product team—not to mention other salespeople who couldn't get products to their customers in time and lost out on sales and commissions. Because of the unforecasted sale, we had to adjust the product order to the factory, which meant that the factory had to step up production. Because the factory couldn't produce fast enough to accommodate all of the orders in time, we had to use air shipping, which was very expensive in comparison to shipping by freighter. The product went on allocation, which meant that other customers who wanted the product couldn't order it easily. All of this affected our market share: since our product wasn't readily available for some time, some of our customers turned to our competitors to fill their immediate needs. My team and I had to explain to executive management why we hadn't been able to better predict the amount of product that we would need from the factory. I still get a sick feeling in my stomach when I think about it.

This whole situation occurred because a salesperson, the account manager for the key customer who placed the large order, was sandbagging. He knew the customer was considering placing an order, but he didn't know with 100 percent certainty and didn't want to be responsible for the forecasted number if the company ended up not placing that order. He also didn't want to explain why he couldn't close the deal if it fell through. So, he didn't list the potential order in his pipeline. He chose to have everyone else deal with a surprise to the upside, rather than take the chance of not making his forecasted potential sales number.

What It Looks Like

While sandbagging is underplaying information, exaggerating is overplaying it. Sandbagging causes rushing that could have been avoided if you had known about the work earlier and prioritized it properly. Exaggeration causes rushing because you think something is happening that really isn't and unnecessarily prioritize certain requests. At the end of the day both sandbagging and exaggerating upset priorities, cause unnecessary haste, and result in extra work for you and your department.

Sandbagging is when a salesperson deliberately gives the perception of underperformance.[9] The term sandbagging may be used differently depending on the profession and job; for instance, in finance it can be used to refer to a stalling tactic,[10] and in law it can refer to intentional silence in the face of potential error.[11] While there seems to be a version of sandbagging in every profession, in this chapter it refers to the situation where salespeople underplay or withhold information so they can keep sales expectations lower or so they won't have to explain to management why a deal fell through. Unfortunately, sandbagging can have a strong negative effect on you and the rest of the marketing team (in addition to people in other departments). A sandbagging salesperson may not tell you until the last minute that she needs materials for an important client meeting because she wasn't sure she would get the meeting.

On the other hand, salespeople may exaggerate information to get you to do what they ask and to prioritize their project. For instance, if you believe a salesperson is close to closing a large deal with a customer, you will do your best to accommodate the sales rep. You might prioritize special requests for custom materials about key solutions, or you might drop everything to create and print signage for sponsorship of the customer's charity golf tournament. You will rush through your priority projects, which can mean working extra hours, paying rush fees, and calling in favors with your team members, agency, or printer. When a large deal is pending, people in all departments do whatever they can to help with the final push to close the sale, and the marketing department is no exception. Because the sale could be the difference between beating quarterly revenue expectations or falling short, you don't want to be the person who didn't try hard enough.

As with sandbagging, exaggerating upsets your project prioritization and causes rushing and extra work that could have been avoided. Believing an upcoming deal is about to close or thinking that a deal will be much bigger than it is changes the way you prioritize your work. The result can range from annoying ("It could have been handled better, but we got the work done without issue") to downright painful ("We stayed here all night to get this done and now we are sleep deprived and our real priorities are suffering").

Salespeople who sandbag and salespeople who exaggerate both cause fire drills for marketing. This type of rushing affects your ability to plan the best way to get work done. I've confirmed with people in other departments that they experience the same behavior when working with salespeople, so it's pervasive and something you should expect.

BEHAVIOR 9: SANDBAGGING AND EXAGGERATING | 123

Here are some examples of sandbagging and exaggeration by salespeople that I've personally experienced:

- A sales VP created a report that allowed him to manipulate what the C-level executives saw. Every month he presented it to executive management, and because he could adjust the numbers, he ensured that executives always saw his results presented in the most positive way. Sometimes he exaggerated the report to make the results seem more positive, and sometimes he held back, sandbagging until the end of the quarter to keep expectations from being too high. When I understood how the VP was using the report, I realized the importance of having access to and using unbiased data sources.

- A salesperson didn't enter his pending deals into the company's CRM tool because he didn't want to be asked questions about progress in sales meetings or have expectations set with management. Instead, he waited until the deals were almost done and then received praise for how quickly he was able to close the sales.

- A sales rep insisted that participation in an upcoming customer event was critical to her business because of the size of a potential deal and the way her customer would react to our participation. Ultimately, our participation was not that important: even though we participated in the customer's event, the deal that closed was much smaller than the salesperson represented.

How to Deal with It

You don't always know if a salesperson is sandbagging or exaggerating, and often you have to act based on what they are telling you, regardless of your suspicion. For example, if you're a product marketing manager and don't take the salesperson at her word regarding the number of units in the pipeline, you could order or manufacture too many or too few of your product and the results will be your fault. However, you can take a few actions to better handle your situation when it comes to these behaviors.

Get Visibility

If you are in marketing, especially product marketing, and you don't have visibility into pending sales deals, you need to find a way to get it. If your company uses a CRM, make your case for getting access to it if you don't already have it. Your ability to check sales pipeline information on a real-time basis is critical when you are planning and forecasting, and it can have real consequences for your entire organization, including the sales team. Having access to the CRM will allow you to have an overview of all deals, even those that are not forecasted to close in the next three to six months or that have a low probability of closing. For example, a report or dashboard may only show you deals with a 50 percent or better probability of closing in the next six months. Being able to see more information on

BEHAVIOR 9: SANDBAGGING AND EXAGGERATING | 125

the CRM—for instance, sales listed with a close probability of 10 percent or a deal that is slated to close in two years—could potentially help you to order enough of a product or plan in advance for account-based marketing activities. For instance, if you get a report that shows deals with the potential to close in the next three to six months, you will only order enough product to fill that need. But if you have visibility to see a large deal that is slated to close in nine months, you may order some of that product early just to hedge against the possibility the order comes in sooner than expected.

If a salesperson comes to you with a request and he has exaggerated information about the size or timeline of his pending deal, you can check the information in your company's CRM and see the listed size, probability, and timeline for the deal prior to directing resources to the request.

If your company doesn't use a CRM, there are still ways to get visibility to the information you need. Some kind of sales pipeline data is produced at your company. Sales managers need this to manage their sales teams. It may be a shared sales spreadsheet or a dashboard that is usually just for sales team members and managers. Invite yourself to sales meetings so that you can hear information about upcoming deals yourself (just start showing up), or start meeting regularly with sales management to check in on deal pipeline information and priorities.

Utilize Historical Information and Analysis

When it comes to forecasting and planning, using historical data is sometimes more accurate than relying on information from sales. Because salespeople could be exaggerating or sandbagging, you might be better off relying on factors like market trends, seasonality, and past activities than on what salespeople are forecasting—as long as you leave a little breathing room for the occasional unplanned deal or activity.

I worked as a product marketing manager at a company where we forecasted units that needed to be manufactured and distributed worldwide. While the company had always relied on sales pipeline data for forecasting, my team took a step back and noted how wildly inaccurate forecasts sometimes were because of factors like sandbagging and exaggerating. So we made a complete change to relying only on historical data, growth models, and seasonality. Once we developed a model, we gave ourselves wiggle room by building in some extra units to have in reserve. Although it wasn't perfect, this strategy was more accurate than past forecasts and moved us away from the swings (and associated anxiety) we experienced when relying on the sales team for information.

You can also apply this principle to marketing activity planning. Look at your department's historical activity and plan for recurring events and campaigns. Track the curve of when you receive requests along with the growth curve of your company or sales team, and make a forecast for activity based on the data. Note the times of year that you receive more requests, for

BEHAVIOR 9: SANDBAGGING AND EXAGGERATING | 127

example, when your customers' business is most active or at the end of their fiscal year. If you've supported marketing programs in the past that didn't show great results, note this information so that you can have criteria and justification for doing it (or not doing it) again if requested. Then, put the data into a plan. It doesn't have to be complicated; it can be a spreadsheet that lists activity on an annual timeline. Build in a little breathing room for emergencies. Then you can act on your plan proactively rather than reacting to requests from sales. When you do get a request from sales, you may already have it in your plan. In addition, it will be easy to make a decision about what you can or can't support, even if the salesperson creates a fire drill because of sandbagging behavior or by using exaggeration.

Behavior 10
Causing Schedule Problems

I worked as a market segment manager at a company with large offices on the West coast and in the Midwest. While I was in the West, most of the salespeople for my market worked out of one of our Midwest offices. As the customer program expert, I was regularly booked on calls with salespeople to talk about the programs we had available. The salesperson would check my schedule, see that I was free, and invite me to her call, along with the customer or partner she was working with. Because of the type of people who were also booked on the calls, I couldn't decline because it would have looked bad. I also knew declining would mean that the salesperson would have to reschedule a meeting that was probably challenging to book in the first place. I was responsible for growing the market segment, and the opportunity to interface with customers, partners, and salespeople was important to me.

The problem was that even though my calendar reflected that I was in California, the salesperson booked me in meetings without regard for the fact that they were often very early or left me with no break in the middle of the day. After a fair amount of frustration (and exhaustion), I knew I had to find a solution.

What It Looks Like

Salespeople who work in the field have more flexible schedules than those of us who are in the office daily. Because of this flexibility, salespeople often adjust their work hours according to what works best for them. For instance, they might read and respond to email at home very early and then get on the road to visit clients. Salespeople can often schedule around personal appointments because they can adjust their start time in the morning or catch up on work in the evening while still working the same number of overall hours.

As a result, salespeople treat scheduling differently than those of us in marketing, and they often unknowingly schedule things in a way that seems discourteous to those of us who follow a typical office worker schedule when arranging calls and meetings.

When preparing to write this book, I interviewed people in both sales and non-sales roles and asked them about different types of scheduling and the associated issues. I found that most non-sales professionals who regularly work with salespeople had experienced issues similar to mine in regard to scheduling with salespeople. At the same time, the salespeople I interviewed were unaware of ever causing scheduling problems for others. I believe this is because an isolated scheduling issue is not that big a deal. It sounds a bit wimpy to respond to a group meeting invitation with a request to start at 8:15 a.m. rather than 8:00 a.m. just because starting at 8:00

sharp means that you'll have to drive in traffic instead of taking your usual train. Because most of us just suck it up and deal with it, the salesperson doesn't realize he is causing inconvenience. Also, it's precisely because salespeople don't regularly work with you in the office that they don't know anything about your schedule the way your other colleagues might. If you work with salespeople a lot, however, the individual scheduling issues that are no big deal as a one-off can accumulate and add up to ongoing frustration.

You can preempt most scheduling issues that will arise by following the recommendations outlined in this chapter. If other non-sales professionals are also being scheduled for meetings and calls with sales, those colleagues will appreciate your effort.

Lunch-Hour Scheduling

As a person who works in the office, you understand that if you don't take a break during the generally accepted lunch hour, you likely won't get a lunch break because you won't be free later. People might schedule you for afternoon meetings or come by your office looking for you, so in general you need to be there. When other office workers schedule meetings, they typically don't schedule them over the lunch hour unless it's a dire circumstance because they have the same issue as you.

Salespeople who work in the field don't understand this concept. They can take lunch whenever they want, and they usually don't stop to consider how scheduling over the lunch hour will upset your day. They don't think of the lunch hour as time you need to sustain yourself, or that you may have plans to pick up a prescription, go to the bank, hit the gym, or actually get something to eat. Sales reps have the freedom to do these things in the margins of their daily appointments, so they don't treat the hour with the same deference as your other coworkers. They see the midday free spot in your calendar and think it's free for them to schedule a meeting.

Mornings and Evenings

You might be the guy who gets in every day at 6:30 a.m., but most marketers, myself included, who work in the office are there during normal business hours. Because many salespeople who work in the field have a home office, they have no problem having a call at 7:30 or 8:00 a.m. They don't think of the fact that if the train is three minutes late, you won't be on a call at exactly 8:00 a.m. or that you'll have to dial in on your mobile phone while trying to negotiate your way into your office building. They don't think of the fact that if you are driving, you have to adjust to traffic patterns and leave your house twenty minutes earlier than usual to ensure you are at your desk at 7:55 a.m. to boot up your computer. Also, the early morning call doesn't give you time to get settled for a few minutes to make sure you are fully prepared. It may mean that you need to skip your morning workout or forgo picking up a really good cup of coffee. Sometimes you can send the salesperson a note about the early call and reschedule for a better time, but you may not want to compromise the way you look to the other people who are scheduled in the meeting. Most people who regularly work in an office are aware that it's better to give people a little leeway in the morning and the evening because they might hit traffic or have to drop off their kids, but it's not something that usually occurs to the salesperson who works in the field.

When you are in the Pacific time zone and the salesperson is in a time zone to the east, it's not uncommon for them to assume you're in the office at an early hour. One salesperson emailed me early in the morning and when I didn't respond within thirty minutes, she escalated the situation to my VP. This all took place within the time frame of my sixty-minute train commute, which unfortunately ran along the coast and took me out of cellular range so there was literally no way I could have seen the communication.

The same issues with morning scheduling generally hold for evening scheduling. Field sales reps don't think of the fact that you have a commuting schedule to stick to, and that participating in calls at close of business day can be a major inconvenience. They don't appreciate the fact that a call that runs over by one minute can cause you to miss your train and then have to wait forty minutes for the next one. They don't understand that if you carpool, a late call on your part can delay the whole group, including the person who needs to get home by a certain time for a child's school play. Having a meeting or call at the very end of the day can cause you to miss your daily workout or have a frustrated spouse at home. Even if you commute by car, a ten-minute difference in the time you get on the road may translate to a thirty-minute difference in the time you have to sit in traffic.

BEHAVIOR 10: CAUSING SCHEDULE PROBLEMS | 133

People who work in the office all the time are sensitive to these morning and evening scheduling issues, and generally don't schedule things right at the beginning or close of business. Instead, they leave a little time for flexibility if they can. Salespeople, however, see a free slot at 8:00 a.m. or 5:00 p.m., and they don't think of how much they may be inconveniencing you and their other coworkers.

Friday Afternoons

In preparing to write this book, I had some frank conversations with sales managers, including one very successful sales manager for a Fortune 100 company. She has managed outside sales reps for over twenty years, and she told me, "Most salespeople just don't work on Friday afternoons. They figure that the week is winding down and it's not a good time to talk to customers anyway, so a lot of them just start their weekend mid-day on Friday."

The funny thing is that when I talked with some of the salespeople who had been on her team and to whom she was referring, they denied the fact that they took Friday afternoons off. I found this to be a common response: sales managers told me their people didn't work on Friday afternoons, and the salespeople who worked for those managers communicated that they did work on Friday afternoons.

The same sales manager told me an amusing story about a sales rep who would purposely leave his jacket on his chair and items like keys or a bag on his desk so that the manager and other people in the sales office would think he was around the office and still working. But the sales rep wasn't actually fooling the manager; she knew he was gone for the weekend. The manager figured it was fine as long as he was making his numbers, so she just let it play out without confrontation.

I know a sales VP who put his office trash can by the copier every Friday afternoon, as opposed to the normal place outside his locked office door, so that he could leave early, and his trash can would still get emptied over the weekend. He thought that because he put it by the copier rather than by his office it wasn't obvious that he had left in the middle of the day.

I've interviewed multiple sales managers as well as other non-sales professionals who regularly work with salespeople, and they all confirm that a lot of salespeople, sales managers, and sales VPs don't work on Friday afternoon. It's part of the culture of the profession. One seasoned sales manager who has managed large sales teams at global companies explained, "We work non-stop during the week, often late into the evening. Sometimes we are traveling as well. So, it makes sense to take off early on Friday afternoon. And, it's generally accepted as something that people in sales do."

It's arguable that salespeople work extra hours during the week. The thing is, other professionals, including those of us in marketing, often do the same without the freedom of movement and flexible schedule that a salesperson might have. Nonetheless, this is the reality of how salespeople see themselves, and the culture of the sales profession is such that salespeople often effectively start their weekend

BEHAVIOR 10: CAUSING SCHEDULE PROBLEMS | 135

midday on Friday. If you try to have a meeting or a call with outside salespeople on Friday afternoon, you are at higher risk of having one of the following issues (all of these have happened to me):

- The salesperson finds a last-minute excuse not to come or call in to your meeting.

- The salesperson doesn't show up because he didn't see the invitation or notification, as he wasn't checking his calendar on Friday afternoon.

- The salesperson calls in to your meeting from her boat, the county fair, or another location that doesn't have great phone service and your call won't be productive.

- The salesperson's head won't be in the game, so he won't be focused, and you will need to later reexplain everything that happened in the meeting or call anyway.

- The salesperson says she needs you to do work over the weekend.

I had a coworker who was working on a project that was critical to a particular salesperson and that had a tight nonnegotiable deadline. My coworker worked late nights during the week and needed to have a meeting Friday afternoon so that he would have direction for what needed to be done over the weekend to meet the Monday project deadline. The salesperson called in to the meeting and his phone kept cutting out because he was on his boat! To my coworker and to the others on the call, it was obvious that the salesperson had started his weekend early while they were putting in extra hours. At the same time, the salesperson perceived that he was working because he had dialed in to the call and didn't imagine that anyone would care that he was on his boat. He was wrong. It irritated everyone; people are still talking about it.

The fact is that most outside salespeople aren't sitting in front of their computer on Friday afternoon, and they aren't really available. While they may check their email and dial in to a call if necessary, you won't have their full attention. By understanding this and proactively dealing with this scheduling issue, you can work more efficiently and successfully with your sales team.

The Monday Meeting Phenomenon

Most salespeople have some sort of Monday sales meeting with their management to go over their pipeline, explain their activities and accomplishments from the previous week, and touch on their plans and pending deals for the upcoming week. If a salesperson isn't making her numbers, she needs to provide an explanation regarding what she is doing to get her numbers up. Although the salesperson will never tell you directly, this is one of the primary reasons that you may get roped in to working late on Friday or over the weekend.

BEHAVIOR 10: CAUSING SCHEDULE PROBLEMS | 137

Because salespeople might need to provide a report detailing their account development and sales pipeline progress during their weekly meeting, they always have an incentive to pressure you into getting work done over the weekend, especially if they didn't have a successful sales week. This creates "I need it for Monday morning" urgency for them, and consequently for you—although sales reps will give you a different reason for the rush. They might tell you it's critical to the customer or needed at an event or sales call, rather than the fact that it will help their presentation if they get called on. If their sales results are lagging, they will be able to use the materials you completed for them to shore up their story to management regarding the work they are doing to develop more business.

As marketing professionals, we tend to take salespeople at their word when they say they need something done before Monday. We don't want to be the reason a customer isn't happy or the reason a deal didn't close, so we will work late on Friday night or even over the weekend to make sure the salesperson has the requested material in time for their deadline. I personally hate having work looming over me during the weekend, so I tend to stay in the office late Friday night and get the work done, rather than be faced with working on Saturday or Sunday. I have worked innumerable late Friday nights. It's frustrating, especially because the late-night work always seems to be for a deadline that the salesperson could have shared earlier. It's likely that the salesperson is just scrambling to be ready for his Monday meeting. It took me a long time to realize this. The

Monday meeting phenomenon has caused me to miss out on many potentially fun Friday nights.

How to Deal with It

I have to admit, scheduling still seems like an area where I'm supposed to suck it up and show up whenever and wherever I'm called upon. I don't want it to seem like work isn't always my priority. In terms of priorities, sleep, exercise, and nourishment should all fall somewhere below work meetings, right? In the past, this perspective led to exhaustion, which ultimately spurred me to develop some practical tactics that help me to shore up the boundaries between work time and personal time. (I hope my boss doesn't read this...)

Take Back Your Lunch Hour

To preserve your lunch break, try creating a recurring meeting on your calendar at noon (or at your preferred lunch time) three to five days a week—depending on how often you are willing to risk someone scheduling over it. On your calendar, you have the option of making the meeting private so that others don't know whether it's a real meeting, appointment, or scheduled break. To hide the fact that you're scheduling an actual lunch break, you can vary the times in your calendar (if you have a job where this is possible), for instance, taking lunch from 12:00 to 1:00 p.m. on one day and 12:30 to 1:30 p.m. the next. You can also schedule it as "tentative" rather than "busy" on your calendar so that if there is something very urgent it can be scheduled over. Creating a lunch-hour appointment will make it more likely that others don't schedule over your lunch time so you can get something to eat, keep your workout schedule (and your sanity), or just get out of the office for a break at least a few days a week.

If you don't want to book a meeting time on your calendar every day, you can simply push back when salespeople try to schedule you during lunch. You can decline the meeting and send a note explaining that you already have plans for lunch that day. It's okay if your plans are just to walk to the local Starbucks; the salesperson doesn't need to know what your plans are. The salesperson is probably not even aware that he is disrupting lunch schedules, so it's a good idea to point that out. The salesperson might complain that it's the only time when everyone is available (which might be true since most people in the office try to keep this time open) and refuse to change it, or she will schedule a different time for the meeting that is less convenient for them, like Friday afternoon.

Another option is to start scheduling salespeople's meetings or calls for them. If you offer to schedule them, sales reps will probably be happy to have you do so. While this may be more work for you up front, you will preempt any back-and-forth communication regarding scheduling issues and you'll ensure the meeting happens at a time that works for you. Keep in mind that salespeople also have times they don't want to schedule, such as Friday afternoons, the last day of the month, or the last week of the quarter. Avoid booking meetings at these times so that you don't create scheduling frustrations for salespeople like they may have created for you in the past.

Avoiding Morning and Evening Scheduling

If you have a strict commuting schedule, put a recurring meeting on your calendar so that you have a little flexibility in the morning when you arrive or in the evening when you need to leave. I know how stressful it is to be scheduled within one minute of when you need to leave the office to catch a train, so use your calendar as a tool to avoid having to deal with this.

Another option is to set up an automatic out-of-office response during your commuting time in the morning and/or evening. You can set it up so it only responds to people in your company and lets them know your status and that you will respond once you are in the office. Outlook allows you to specify responses for inside your company versus outside your company, and you can even include rules to exclude key people, such as executives, from receiving your out-of-office response. This can help hold off salespeople who may escalate requests if they don't get a response from you right away.

Alternatively, you can choose to ignore communication from your sales team until you get in the office in the morning and after you need to leave in the evening. In this way you are creating a boundary for yourself around your business hours. It may take the sales team a while to catch on, but if they deal with you enough, they will eventually get the message. If you do this, don't deviate from your business-hours strategy, even if you are in the office earlier or later. Once salespeople realize they can reach you or schedule you outside of your office hours, they may expect to be able to do it all the time.

In the situation at the beginning of the chapter where salespeople were scheduling meetings during any free time in my calendar, I solved the problem by booking my own recurring meetings during times I didn't want to be scheduled, including 6:00 a.m. to 8:00 a.m. daily.

Forget Friday Afternoons

The solution to this problem is simple: don't schedule anything with salespeople on Friday afternoons, not so they can have their weekend start early, but rather so you can avoid potential frustration. Although Friday afternoon may look like a good time to schedule meetings because salespeople don't have appointments on their calendar, you will likely experience the issues that come along with Friday afternoon scheduling, so better to simply avoid it.

Beware the Monday Meeting Phenomenon

By Friday, if their sales didn't come through during the week, salespeople will be getting concerned about having something to talk about in their Monday meeting. If you talk to a salesperson before Friday, you still have time during the work week to help them with last-minute requests. If you meet with them on Friday, you'll be more likely to work late on Friday or over the weekend.

The Monday meeting phenomenon is another reason to avoid Friday meetings and calls with salespeople. If a salesperson still makes a request on Friday to get some work done before Monday, push back. Remind the salesperson of the lead time needed for project requests and suggest a reasonable deadline date for his request. If he counters with a compelling reason such as a client meeting or presentation, remember that the salesperson's job is overcoming objections and he may be making the request seem more important than it really is—there isn't a way for you to know for sure. You can respond with a legitimate explanation of your own, for instance, you may you need to get management approval to spend time on the project, you may be planning to go out of town over the weekend, or you may have no time to spare because you are currently on a deadline for another project. If you can get the work done without too much inconvenience, absolutely go ahead and help the salesperson—there isn't anything wrong with helping someone when you can. Don't, however, say you can do a project by their deadline and then change your mind because you over-promised; this will only hurt your reputation. It would be better to give the salesperson a more realistic picture of your ability to meet his request.

CONCLUSION

Salespeople aren't the enemy, and working with them isn't always about dealing with problems. When you as a marketer work in sync with salespeople to introduce products, implement programs, and promote new business, you'll both be successful, and the results of your work will be felt throughout your entire organization. While understanding the pitfalls of working with salespeople will help you to stay on track and achieve your daily goals, working well with salespeople is one of the most important things you can do to achieve overall success in your current role and in your career.

Some of the best marketers, myself included, have spent time as part of the sales organization in a business development, sales, or sales management role. Taking the time to understand the sales process from the perspective of a salesperson can provide you with firsthand insight into why salespeople sometimes act the way they do. They are often in a high-pressure situation where they have to close a certain amount of business within a limited time frame to earn their commission, pay their bills, and even keep their job. If you get the chance, even if it's for a limited time, consider working in a sales organization to gain perspective that will ultimately help you to achieve your long-term marketing career goals.

    Just as some of the best marketing professionals have spent time in the sales organization, some of the best salespeople have spent time working in marketing. Having this background gives sales reps a better ability to communicate with the marketing organization and to understand how to best take advantage of programs and materials. If you can find a person in your sales organization with a marketing background, you may be able to partner with him to pilot new programs, test campaign effectiveness, and tailor programs in a way that will achieve better sales results. Working together will give the salesperson the advantage of leveraging new programs and materials while simultaneously making you a more successful marketer. Seek out salespeople with a marketing background and make an effort to work with them.

    I hope you use this book to recognize, understand, and have a strategy to respond to some of the common salesperson behaviors that frustrate marketing professionals. By knowing what to expect and how to respond, you can avoid becoming upset when salespeople act in certain ways. You can also avoid being manipulated by salesperson behavior and possibly use your understanding of the situation to work more effectively with your sales team, increase your efficiency, remain focused, and ultimately become more productive. Using the advice in this book can also help you to stay fixed on your priorities in other circumstances, such as when you are faced with new management, executive requests, and even distractions within your own department. At the end of the day, you'll be judged on what you've achieved, the success of your programs, and how you're perceived by others. Working well with salespeople will help you accomplish results faster, create successful outcomes, and achieve your career goals.

Acknowledgments

Thank you to all the people who answered my many questions, took part in surveys, spent time being interviewed, and gave me feedback, insights, and impressions so that I could write this book. I appreciate all your help, inspiration and encouragement, including especially Tom Hicks, Paul Mecklenburg, Thor Mecklenburg, Alida Tustison, Joe Chotirawi, Gail Fay, Mariella Palmer, Adam Hanin, Pat Shaw, Mark Middendorf, Rob Motley, Kristen Mathews, Will Casavan, Jim Palmer, Eileen Kawakami Wilson, Fanny Guerra Kuperstein, Keith Tague, Rafael Bretado, Nick Chiew, Pam Wiles Rivero, Scott Philips, Lily Mamola, Jack McDaniel, Dave Stark, Sam Hughes, Ryan Andrews, Jami Fronk, Paul Collas, Kush Kapila, Pete Kaczmarek, Juan Vargas, Béatrice Juquelier, Luigi Amoretti, Kelsey Elcome, Ron Gillies, Marlon Woolforde, Ryan Nichols, Jack McDaniel, Tom Duong, Jody Krimstock, Al Brunelle, Angelina Scott, Miki Barr, Daniel Woodward, Alain Mazer, Ryan Sasscer, Marni Kintner, and Thor Holt.

End Notes

[1] Ian Heller, president and COO, Modern Distribution Management, from RA partner marketing conference presentation, Milwaukee, WI, October 3, 2018.

[2] Philip Kotler, Neil Rackham, and Suj Krishnaswamy, "Ending the War between Sales and Marketing," Harvard Business Review, July-August 2006, https://hbr.org/2006/07/ending-the-war-between-sales-and-marketing.

[3] Steven Altman, Enzo Valenzi, Richard M Hodgetts, Organizational Behavior: Theory and Practice (Orlando, FL: Academic Press, Inc., 1985), 115–117.

[4] Andy Smith, "Rapport," Practical NLP Podcast, November 26, 2013, https://nlppod.com/

[5] Robert B. Cialdini, Influence: The Psychology of Persuasion (New York, HarperCollins, 2009), 115.

[6] Robert B. Cialdini, Influence: The Psychology of Persuasion (New York, HarperCollins, 2009), 17.

[7] Chase Hughes, The Ellipsis Manual: Analysis and Engineering of Human Behavior (Virginia Beach, VA, Evergreen Press, 2017), 118–120.

[8] S. Milgram, "Behavioral Study of Obedience," Journal of Abnormal and Social Psychology 67, no. 4 (1963): 376 – 377.

[9] Wikipedia, s.v. "Sandbagging," https://en.wikipedia.org/wiki/Sandbagging.

[10] The Free Dictionary , s.v., "Sandbag," https://financial-dictionary.thefreedictionary.com/sandbagging.

[11] Bryn Kirvin, "To Sandbag or Not to Sandbag," San Diego CountyBar Association, https://www.sdcba.org/index.cfm?pg=Ethics - in - Brief -- 4 - 14 - 2014.

About the Author

TASHA HICKS is an award-winning marketer who has worked in companies ranging from small to Fortune 100. With experience in all things marketing including managing market segments, products, trade shows, communications, programs, digital and marketing teams, and with titles that range from Associate to Director, she's also held roles as a business development executive and inside sales manager. Originally from Seattle, Tasha received her BA from the University of Southern California and MBA from Pepperdine University. She lives in Oceanside, California with her husband Tom and her cat Livingston. SURVIVING SALESPEOPLE is her first book.

Thank You

Thank you for reading my book. If you enjoyed SURVIVING SALESPEOPLE, please consider leaving a review wherever you purchased your copy.

To learn more about the book or to connect with me, please visit www.survivingsalespeople.com.

www.ingramcontent.com/pod-product-compliance
Lightning Source LLC
Chambersburg PA
CBHW071407210526
45465CB00001B/294